The Boy to Man Book

PREPARING YOUR SON FOR MANHOOD

DEDICATION

To Jonathan David Fischer
A son to be proud of

"A wise son makes a glad father." ~ Proverbs 10:1

Contents

Introduction for Fathers
This book is about becoming a real man.

There is a crying need for a strong masculine presence in our homes, our churches, our communities, and our nation today. We have become feminized as a culture, and the muscular strength which is needed to protect our values, our culture, and even our daughters has been bled away.

Young women, eager to take refuge under the protection of a strong husband, can't find one. Some even despair, and either figure they will go unmarried for life or have to settle.

Where do the men of tomorrow come from?

Well, Dad, you are raising one of them right now. You are shaping an arrow in your quiver, preparing it for flight.

There is only one place we are going to find the men our nation will need in the years to come: they must come from the homes of today. Not from our churches, although the church clearly has a role. Not from our schools, which have abandoned character instruction altogether. Not from youth organizations, as helpful as they may be, for the simple reason that no one can replace a father in a young boy's life.

The bottom line is that America is looking to the dads of today for the strong men of tomorrow.

This book is addressed to your son, but is designed for you to read with your son between his 12th and 13th birthdays, which was the customary age at which a Jewish boy became a "son of the law," the literal meaning of the phrase "bar-mitzvah."

It was at age 12 that Jesus was first found in the Temple, "sitting among the teachers, listening to them and asking them questions" (Luke 2:46). Why was he there? Because he had become a "son of the law" and now had the responsibility to follow the law which required all adult males to travel to Jerusalem for the three annual feasts.

A Jewish boy at age 12 was no longer considered a child. He was a young man, and was expected to accept adult responsibilities and live no longer as a child but as a man.

In our culture, which has celebrated prolonged adolescence and turned it into a virtual art form, it's long past time for us to challenge our young boys to see themselves as young men and act accordingly.

This book is designed to help you firmly establish your own son in the timeless wisdom of Solomon. It's designed to help you put him on a glide path to independence and maturity as he prepares to leave home and take his own place in the world.

I was struck several years ago with a sudden and eye-opening realization that the book of Proverbs is a training manual for fathers. No less than 23 times in this book, Solomon addresses his words to "my son." It is a distillation of the wisdom the wisest man who ever lived was eager to impart to his own son.

So while there are many uses to which the book of Proverbs may be put, there is no use that is more important than its original one: to help dads raise masculine, mature, muscular, and godly sons.

As you read this book to your son, and pray the truth of the Word of God into his life, it is my hope that God will use the words on these pages to make a lifelong difference in his life. The woman he marries and the sons they bear together will be eternally grateful that you cared enough to "train up a child in the way he should go" (Prov. 22:6).

The Fear of the Lord

CHAPTER 1

**A mature young man loves the Lord with all his heart;
an immature boy doesn't.**

*"The fear of the LORD is the beginning of knowledge; fools
despise wisdom and instruction." ~ Proverbs 1:7*

A man got lost in the English countryside, and stopped to
ask a local farmer how to get to London. "Well," said the farmer, "If I was going to London, I wouldn't start from here."

If you are going to get where you want to go in life, you
have to start at the right place. And the right place to start
is to have a strong relationship with God. Building a strong
relationship with God is the single most important thing you
will ever do in your life.

When the book of Proverbs talks about "knowledge," it's
talking about having the only kind of knowledge that's important to be successful in life.

Now you will run into a lot of people on your way to becoming a man who will tell you they have the knowledge you
need. But if you want to have the only kind of knowledge
that counts, the kind of knowledge that will turn you from
a young man into a strong, mature man, you have to start at
the right place. And the place you have to start is with the
"fear of the LORD."

When the Bible talks about the "fear of the LORD," it does
not mean that we have to be afraid of God like we would be
afraid of a bad man. It means simply that we must have a

deep respect for God and honor him more than anyone or anything else in the universe.

Having a strong relationship with God is much more important in life than having the right friends, marrying the right girl, getting the right education, or getting the right job.

The word "wisdom" in the Hebrew language literally means "skill." God wants you to have the skills that are necessary to build the kind of life you want and that he desires for you. And to acquire that wisdom, that skill, you must begin with the fear of the Lord. There is no other place to start. If you start anywhere else, you will not get where you want to go in life.

As you get older, you will run into more and more people who will despise the wisdom of the Bible. This will be especially true if you go to college. Some of these people will be highly educated, and they will be quite proud of the fact that they have rejected God and his truth. And they will try to get you to believe that only people who aren't very smart still believe the Bible.

You may have teachers in high school and you will have professors in college who will ridicule the Scriptures and ridicule anyone who believes them. You must make up your mind right now that you will not be fooled by these people. The mark of a fool is that he is naive and will believe anything he is told. Do not let these people who think they are so smart deceive you. They do not have your best interests at heart. People who are easily swayed are fools. Don't be a fool!

You must never forget that the real fool is the man who rejects God, not the man who honors him. Never, ever forget that "the fear of the LORD is the beginning of wisdom."

A Father's Prayer

Father, I pray that my son will always remember that fearing you, revering you, respecting you, and honoring you is the beginning of knowledge. Make him strong when others try to fool him into rejecting you and your Word. Make him strong in his faith so that he may acquire the full measure of the knowledge that will make him a mature man. In Jesus' name, Amen.

Your Father's Wisdom

CHAPTER 2

**A mature young man listens to his father's counsel;
an immature boy doesn't.**

*"Hear, my son, your father's instruction, and forsake not your
mother's teaching, for they are a graceful garland for your head
and pendants for your neck." ~ Proverbs 1:8-9*

As you grow toward manhood over the next few years, you
will run into more and more people who will try to convince
you that your father doesn't know what he's talking about.

They will try to get you to believe that the values he is trying to instill in you are old-fashioned and out-of-date. You
will run across a lot of people - friends, teachers, professors,
voices on social media and on television - who will have
nothing but contempt for the values we are talking about
here together.

If you listen to them, they just might persuade you to dump
these values and adopt theirs, values which just might destroy
your life. Do not let them do this to you.

Your father loves you far more than they do. He loves you
more than he loves his own life. He would lay down his life
for you in a heartbeat without even having to think about it
because he loves you so much. The folks who will try to get
you to reject his values don't love you like that.

The values he is trying to teach you are a protection for you.
They point to a pathway that will lead to life, happiness, and

prosperity. It's a path your dad wants you to walk because he wants only the best for you.

There were times - by God's grace they were few and far between - when I had to tell my son J.D., "No." It might have been over something his friends were allowed to do but which I didn't think was good for him, or some privilege they had that I didn't think was right for him, or extending curfew beyond what his mom and I didn't think was wise. This understandably didn't make him very happy, and so one night I explained it this way to him: "J.D., my job as your father is not to give you a happy childhood. My job as your father is to raise you to be a responsible and mature adult."

Then when I got to the door of his bedroom on my way out, I turned back to him. "By the way, in case this question ever comes up in the future, you are having a happy childhood."

Don't let yourself be tricked into rejecting your father's values by somebody who tries to impress you with how much smarter they are than your father. If they try to get you to throw the values we are talking about into the trash, they are the ones who do not know what they are talking about.

It's because these values are not just your father's values. They come from the heart and mind of God himself. To reject these values is not just to reject your father's wisdom, it is to reject the wisdom of God. Don't make that mistake.

Solomon urged his son to wear the words of wisdom he heard from his father around his neck like a necklace which he never takes off but wears all the time. The wisdom that is found on the end of that necklace lies over your heart. It's Solomon's way of telling you to take these values and store them up in your heart and never forget them.

Here's a quote attributed to Mark Twain:

When I was a boy of 14, my father was so ignorant I could hardly stand to have the old man around. But when I got to be 21, I was astonished at how much the old man had learned in seven years.

The point, here, of course, is that it wasn't Twain's father who got smarter over those seven years, but Twain himself. What Mark Twain meant is that he had come to understand as a man how right his father's counsel had been all along and how foolish he had been to reject it in his teenage years. The older you get, the smarter your dad will be. Start learning from him right now.

Let me finish this conversation with the words of Scripture, the words of a loving father speaking with his son.

"My son, do not forget my teaching, but let your heart keep my commandments, for length of days and years of life and peace they will add to you." ~ Proverbs 3:1-2

A FATHER'S PRAYER
Father, I pray that my son will embrace the values of your Word and never forget them as long as he lives. I claim your promise that you will grant him life and peace as a reward for following you. In Jesus' name, amen.

Friends

CHAPTER 3

**A mature young man chooses his friends carefully;
an immature boy does not.**

"If you lie down with dogs, you get up with fleas."
~ *modern proverb*

"Bad company ruins good character."
~ *1 Corinthians 15:33 (NIV)*

The most important decision you are going to make in the next few years is your choice of friends. As Solomon says, "The righteous choose their friends carefully, but the way of the wicked leads them astray" (Prov. 12:26, ESV footnote).

A boy is sometimes careless about his choice of friends, and will run with a group of friends who will get him into trouble. In fact, the quickest way for you to get in trouble and get off in the weeds is to hang with the wrong crowd.

There are a lot of things worse than spending Friday night at home with your parents, and one of them is rolling with a group of guys who will take you places you do not want to go.

In contrast, a young man on his way to mature manhood picks his friends very carefully, and only runs with those who are making good life decisions and moving in the same direction he wants to go.

Solomon says, "A righteous man is cautious in friendship, but the way of the wicked leads them astray" (Prov. 12:26, NIV). I can't tell you how many guys out there who are basically good guys but got hooked up with the wrong circle of friends. They wound up getting pulled into stuff that left them either in big trouble or going nowhere in life.

Author and motivational speaker Steve Maraboli put it this way: "If you surround yourself with clowns, don't be surprised when your life resembles a circus." This is what Solomon wanted his son to learn: "Whoever walks with the wise becomes wise, but the companion of fools will suffer harm" (Prov. 13:20).

On the other hand, if you "walk with the wise" as Solomon suggests, if you "choose your friends carefully," you'll be surrounded by guys who will make you a better man and keep you out of trouble.

My best friend in high school, Wayne, shared my faith and values, and we shared some of the same interests. For instance, we played high school basketball together. We enjoyed a terrific friendship, made good choices, had fun, and stayed out of trouble.

When I got to college at Stanford, I tried out for the freshman basketball team as a walk-on. I got cut, which was no surprise to people who had seen me play, but before I got cut, one day at practice I met the guy, Bruce, who became my best friend through college and beyond. He played high school basketball, by the way, with Bill Walton, who became a famous center at UCLA and then in the NBA.

Anyway, Bruce and I struck up a fast friendship and hung out together. We soon got to know a man by the name of Paul, a guy who was a little bit older and was doing an internship at Peninsula Bible Church. He'd been assigned to the Stanford campus.

Paul began meeting three days a week in the morning with Bruce and me for Bible study, discipleship and prayer. This went on for both our freshman and sophomore years. Those two years were probably the most important years of my life in terms of locking down the spiritual and moral values that would guide me for the rest of my life. Bruce and I stayed in contact with each other long past our shared college experience. In fact, he was the best man at my wedding.

And Paul performed the wedding ceremony for me and my bride. Friends matter.

I pledged a fraternity - a good one - at the end of my freshman year. I helped co-lead a Bible study there that eventually had almost a third of the frat guys in it. In fact, the rest of the guys called a special meeting one time because they were afraid we were trying to turn the fraternity into a Christian theme-house!

Solomon says, "A man of many companions may come to ruin, but there is a friend who sticks closer than a brother" (Prov. 18:24).

Look for a friend like that, pray for a friend like that, and don't rest until you find a friend like that. And perhaps most importantly, be a friend like that. You'll never regret it.

Motivational speaker John Kuebler put it this way, "Show me your friends, and I'll show you your future." Make sure you choose quality friends. Starting today.

A FATHER'S PRAYER

Father, I pray that you will bring good, godly friends into my son's life who will help him and encourage him as he grows to maturity. And I pray that you will make him a friend like that to others. By your grace, may he know the blessing of close, godly, masculine friendship in the years to come. In Jesus' name, amen.

Your Closest Friends

CHAPTER 4

**A mature young man runs with the right crowd;
an immature young man doesn't.**

"A friend loves at all times, and a brother is born for adversity."
~ *Proverbs 17:17*

*"A man of many companions may come to ruin, but there is a
friend who sticks closer than a brother."* ~ *Proverbs 18:24*

"Iron sharpens iron, and one man sharpens another."
~ *Proverbs 27:17*

There are few decisions you make in life that will be more
important than the close friends you make and keep.

I'm not talking here about acquaintances, but rather males
with whom you spend your free time. These are the guys with
whom you go to the movies, play softball, hunt, and grab a
burger at the local sports restaurant. These are the guys you
go to church with, and the guys that are a part of your small
group fellowship.

These are the men who become your closest friends. You
will have casual relationships with a lot of different people,
but you've only got room in your life for just a few really good
buddies. Who these guys are will have a lot to do with the
kind of man you become. Be sure you choose carefully and
well, starting right now.

This is what Solomon means when he says, "A righteous
man is cautious in friendship, but the way of the wicked leads

them astray" (Prov. 12:26, NIV). A man chooses his friends very carefully because he knows that picking the wrong buddies can be a disaster.

Even Jesus Christ himself trusted very few men in his life. The Bible says, "Jesus on his part did not entrust himself to them (his fan club), because he knew all people and needed no one to bear witness about man, for he himself knew what was in man" (John 2:24-25). This doesn't mean he was paranoid or suspicious. He was just careful.

He had twelve close friends (the disciples), three very close friends (Peter, James and John), and one best friend (John, whom the Bible describes as "the disciple whom Jesus loved").

You want to pick friends you admire for their intelligence, their values, and their character. You will learn from them, and each one will make you a better man. A man with strong character will draw you up to his level, while a man with weak character will pull you down to his.

Solomon puts it this way: "He who walks with the wise grows wise, but a companion of fools suffers harm" (Prov. 13:20 NIV). Wisdom rubs off, and so does stupidity.

Now of course it's possible for a guy to be both popular and mature, which means he'll be a good influence on the cool kids who hang with him.

But a lot of popular guys have pretty lousy character, and that ought to be a warning sign to you to steer clear. It's easy to think that hanging around with popular guys or cool guys with bad character won't get you in trouble, but it sure can and it sure will.

Trust me, you will never regret being cautious and careful in your choice of friends. I think of the good friends I've had over the course of my life, and what they have meant to me.

Wayne taught me you can have a whole lot of fun without getting into trouble. Bruce taught me the incredible importance of having a strong Christian buddy in a hostile and secular environment. I loved playing basketball with Bruce and sharing his robust sense of humor. Jeff strengthened my faith while we were in grad school together.

Ray instilled in me a love of muscular Christianity and mentored me during our weekly round of golf. David instilled in me a love for the Word of God. Paul taught me the importance of small group discipleship.

Bob was there for me at a very uncertain time in my professional career. Tim showed up one night at just the right time to steady my hand in the middle of a crisis.

Vacationing at different times with Jim and Howard and Don and Kevin and their families was just a blast, as we reinforced our love for our wives and our children. Henry and I developed a close friendship through hitting the links together. Tim shared my love of golf and public policy, and I valued the golf and the conversation every time we hauled out the sticks. Each one of these men has played a treasured and irreplaceable role in my life, and each, in his own way, strengthened my grip on God.

There's a perfect example of this in the Bible. At a critical time in David's life, his best buddy Jonathan found him in the wilderness, on the run from Jonathan's own father, Saul, who was trying to kill David. Here's what the Bible says: "Jonathan, Saul's son, rose and went to David at Horesh, and strengthened his hand in God" (1 Samuel 23:16).

May God bless you with friends like that, as he did me, and may you be a friend like that to others.

Solomon says as iron sharpens iron, so one man sharpens

another. If you want a sharp blade on a knife or a sword or an axe or even a lawn-mower, you have to sharpen that blade. That requires friction and friction produces sparks.

Some close friends will challenge you in your thinking and in your decision-making. That's all good. When those sparks fly, it means one thing: God is using them to shape and sharpen your character.

A FATHER'S PRAYER

Father, I pray that you will bless my son with close friends who will strengthen his grip on you. As iron sharpens iron, I pray that they will help shape him into a mature man who can be an instrument in your hands. Help him to choose his close friends wisely and carefully. In Jesus' name, amen.

Trust in the Lord

CHAPTER 5

A boy trusts in himself; a real man trusts in God.

"Trust in the Lord with all your heart, and do not lean on your own understanding. In all your ways acknowledge him, and he will make straight your paths." ~ Proverbs 3:5-6

As you head toward adult manhood, one of the most important questions you have to answer is this: "Whom am I depending on to get me where I want to go?"

You have dreams and desires even right now about what you want your adult life to be. Those dreams include what kind of man you want to become, dreams about getting married and building a family, and dreams about building a fulfilling career.

In pursuing those dreams, you will have to depend on someone or something to help you. Ultimately, you have only two choices: to depend upon God and his wisdom or depend upon yourself and your own wisdom.

The counseling of God's Scripture is this: "Trust in the LORD with all your heart" and "in all your ways acknowledge him." This means to count on him completely, for everything and in everything. For strength, for direction, for guidance, for assistance, for wisdom, and for the counsel to make good decisions.

If you trust in the Lord with all your heart, you have his promise that he "will make straight your paths." That is, he will show you the direction to take in your life. Where to go to college, whom to date, whom to marry, what career to pursue, where to live, when to start a family, when to change jobs. A multitude of very, very important decisions lie ahead of you in your life, and if you want to make the right call each time it's imperative that you trust in God and his wisdom at every step.

It's a weak analogy, but God is a bit like a GPS satellite. When people depend upon a GPS system, they use a device that sends a signal to a very complex processor that is so far above them in the heavens that they can't even see it. But the satellite receives that signal and returns a signal to earth that enables a driver to find that pizza place or movie theater he's looking for.

Depending on that heavenly guidance system beats driving around aimlessly, trusting your own instincts and hoping you will eventually stumble across your destination by chance.

Solomon tells you not "to lean on your own understanding." To lean on something means to place your weight on it, to trust it to support you. Leaning on your own understanding is to place your weight on something that may look sturdy but isn't strong enough to support you in the end.

Not too long ago, the news carried a story about the second story floor of a building that gave way because it couldn't hold the weight of everybody who was upstairs. A lot of people were injured in the collapse. Your own understanding is a lot like that floor. If you lean on your own understanding, even though it looks like something solid, you will wind up just like those folks, falling through the floor and landing in a heap. Don't let this happen to you.

Instead, "Trust in the Lord with all your heart, and do not lean on your own understanding. In all your ways acknowledge him and he will make straight your paths." He will get you where you want to go and make you the man you want to be.

A Father's Prayer

Father, I pray that my son will learn to trust in you with all of his heart, and learn to depend on your understanding and wisdom instead of his own. I pray that as he does, you will go before him, make his paths straight and fulfill every purpose you have for his life. In Jesus' name, amen.

Be a Faithful Friend

CHAPTER 6

A boy is a fickle friend; a real man is a faithful friend.

"A friend loves at all times, and a brother is born for adversity."
~ Proverbs 17:17

There is nothing quite as important in life as having a small set of friends who are loyal to you to the end. And there's nothing quite as important as being that kind of friend to others.

True friends are loyal to you when you're up, when you're down, when you succeed, when you fail, when the world praises you and when the world condemns you. Being a true friend means friends can count on you when they need you the most.

And on the other hand, there is nothing quite so painful as to be abandoned in a time of crisis by someone you thought was a friend.

Some of the deepest pain I have experienced in my life has been at the hands of men I thought were true friends but who turned on me in betrayal right when I needed a "friend who loves at all times."

But some of the richest experiences of my life have come when good men have come to my side when others had rejected me.

I remember in particular one incident about a year after I had started a new church. After a showdown took place at a board meeting over a biblical matter on which I could not compromise, the other members of the membership team left en masse just two or three short days later. It left me alone at a time when their resignations could have been fatal for the life of that young church.

Their departure rocked me hard for many reasons, not the least of which was that the church was my only source of income to take care of my young family. And my income that first year was quite modest to begin with.

At that time, our worship team rehearsed on Thursday nights, and it happened to be on a Thursday night that I got the phone call informing me that I was now in this thing all by myself.

While I was still absorbing the blow, pondering matters while cleaning up dishes in the kitchen sink, I noticed a car pull up in front of the house. Out stepped the drummer on our worship band, who just happened to stop by on his way home from rehearsal. This, as I remember, was the only time he was prompted to drop by the house unannounced just to see how I was doing.

He came in, grabbed a seat, and when I informed him of what had just happened, he could readily see that it had shaken me up. His response to it all was just what I needed to hear. I do not remember the exact words he used, but I remember as if it were yesterday how timely they were and how much I needed to hear his words of encouragement and hope. He truly was a "brother born for adversity."

I spent the next day in prayer and fasting. I took a long hike around a mountain called Shaffer Butte that hovers above the city of Boise. As I spent that time listening to God in the quiet and beauty of his creation, seven names came into mind as the best choices to become our new elders. That very next Sunday I asked the congregation's help in replacing the leadership team of the church. They turned in secret ballots with names on them, and by God's grace their top seven names were identical to the seven names that had pressed themselves into my mind during my day alone with God. We wound up with seven men of maturity and wisdom and a much stronger and seasoned elder board than we had had just days before.

Solomon says, "A man of many companions may come to ruin, but there is a friend who sticks closer than a brother" (Prov. 18:24). In other words, you may find in time that the brothers you have in Christ become even closer to you than the brothers who are a part of your own family.

It's far better to have a handful of dependable friends, even only one, than a whole posse of guys who can't be counted on when the chips are down. Choose your friends wisely.

How do you find friends like this? That's easy: be a friend like this. Make it your goal to be a "friend (who) loves at all times," a "brother born for adversity," a "friend who sticks closer than a brother," and it won't be long before you will have some good buds around you who will return the favor.

We call our son J.D., but his full name is Jonathan David. We gave him that name in honor of the Jonathan and David in the Bible, who developed one of the richest male friendships in the Bible. We named him that because it was our hope and prayer that he would grow up to be the kind of friend to others that Jonathan and David were to each other - faithful, loyal, and dependable. By God's grace, he has grown into a man just like that. That's just the kind of man your father wants you to become.

When J.D. was in high school, he befriended an underclassman who was a refugee from Afghanistan. Almaz had a sunny disposition, but he was slight in build and was a special needs student. He was the type of guy that bullies like to pick on. He attached himself to J.D. because J.D. was one of the few guys on campus that treated him with unfailing kindness.

One day, while J.D. was walking down a hallway, he saw another student throw Almaz to the floor and do an "elbow drop" on him, a professional wrestling move where you drop on a guy that's flat on his back and punch him in the stomach with your elbow. The bully's friends thought the whole thing was funny and laughed. Almaz got up off the floor and tried to shake it off, but my son could see the raw pain in his eyes. It infuriated J.D. He grabbed the bully and literally shoved him up against the lockers, got right in his grill, and said, "If you ever want to touch Almaz like that again, you are going to have to go through me." Almaz never had to worry again about being picked on. I'm not sure I have ever been prouder of my son than I was that day.

A Father's Prayer

Father, I pray that my son will grow up to be a friend who loves at all times, a friend who is born for adversity, and a friend who sticks closer than a brother. I pray that you will bring into his life men who will be his faithful and loyal friends in return. As you knit the soul of Jonathan together with David, so I pray that you will knit his soul together with the friends of your choosing. In Jesus' name, Amen.

Listen to your Friends

CHAPTER 7

A boy gets angry when his friends tell him the truth; a real man listens and grows from it.

"Faithful are the wounds of a friend." ~ Proverbs 27:6a

"As iron sharpens iron, so one man sharpens another."
~ Proverbs 27:17 (NIV)

It's important to develop friendships with men who will tell you the truth. And it's important that you learn to listen to them when they do.

None of us see ourselves with perfect clarity. We are blind to many of our own shortcomings and weaknesses. Others can see them but we can't. We are so oblivious to our own flaws that we often just don't see them even when they are glaringly obvious to others.

So we have to learn how to listen to others, ask them for their opinions, and be willing to consider seriously what they say. They certainly will not be infallible, and so you don't have to accept everything they say without question, but they will see things about you that you will not see.

We're also very quick to justify our own behavior and speech. Everything we do will seem right in our own eyes at the time we do it. And if it's in some situation that is emotionally charged, the chances are even higher that we will defend ourselves to the hilt and find it hard to accept the possibility that we might be at fault.

All this explains why we need male friends who will tell us the truth about ourselves.

Solomon says, "Wounds from a friend can be trusted, but an enemy multiplies kisses" (Prov. 27:6 NIV).

Another translation says, "Faithful are the wounds of a friend." "Faithful" means trustworthy or dependable. They are words you can count on, words you can lean on and place your weight on.

Because they come from a friend, you know his words, as hard as they may be to hear at times, come from someone who loves you and cares about you and wants only the best for you. Listen to a friend like that, even when his words are difficult to hear.

Now Solomon says they are "wounds." That means when friends tell you the truth, it might hurt. And you'll find yourself reacting defensively and wanting to dismiss what they tell you because all of us find it difficult to admit to ourselves that we've blown it.

But a real man will resist the impulse to reflexively defend himself. Receive what you hear from friends, weigh it, think it over, ask God to help you sort through what you've heard, and then hang on to the truth of what they've told you.

Eric, a very good friend, once took me aside for a private chat, and said, "Bryan, it seems to me like your heart is like a shed in the corner of your backyard. It's a dark shed, and you've got the door to that shed padlocked. And you've locked it because there's a lot of dark stuff in there, inside that locked up shed, that you don't want to look at. You need to unlock that door and let God start pulling the stuff that's in there out into the light so he can help you deal with it. If you don't, it's going to hurt you and it's going to hurt other people in your life."

You think I wanted to hear that? Nope. But my friend was right, and he put me on a journey of allowing God to examine my heart that has lasted to this very day. I needed to hear that message from a trusted friend, and he gave it to me. It wasn't fun, but it was a life-giving message.

Solomon also says, "Perfume and incense bring joy to the heart, and the pleasantness of one's friend springs from his earnest counsel" (Prov. 27:9 NIV). When a friend is speaking to you sincerely and thoughtfully, you'd best listen. The best friends you will ever have are the ones who will speak truth into your life.

One of the most familiar of all the proverbs is this one: "As iron sharpens iron, so one man sharpens another" (Prov. 27:17 NIV). As mentioned before, sharpening a blade, whether on a knife or a mower, requires friction and that friction produces sparks. But that's the only way a blade can become as sharp as it needs to be to do all it was designed to do.

So in your friendship with close male friends, there may be times of friction and times when the sparks fly. But that is how God is preparing you to be a sharp instrument in his hand. You can't cut wood with a dull axe.

A FATHER'S PRAYER

Father, I pray that you will make my son into a man who is willing to receive the truth from his friends, even when it is hard to hear. And use him to speak a word of truth into the lives of his friends when they need to hear it. In Jesus' name, amen.

The Word of God is Flawless

CHAPTER 8

A boy does not believe in the absolute authority of the Word of God; a real man does.

"Every word of God proves true; he is a shield to those who take refuge in him. Do not add to his words, lest he rebuke you and you be found a liar." ~ Proverbs 30:5-6

As you grow into manhood, you will hear a lot of people make claims that what they are saying is right and true and something that everybody should believe. But many of these things will contradict things that other people say with the same amount of confidence and authority.

How can you know who is telling you the truth and who isn't?

We lived in a home once where a previous do-it-yourself owner had added a wing to the house. The door jambs were crooked. From a distance, they looked fine, but when you looked at them more closely it was easy to see that the outer jambs weren't strictly parallel with each other, and the top jamb wasn't strictly parallel with the floor. This meant that the door didn't fit. There were gaps at the top of the door, and along the sides of the door, all of which let in cold air during winter and hot air during summer.

How do expert carpenters avoid errors like that? They use what is called a level, usually two to four feet long, and made of wood with a sealed glass or plastic tube right in the middle. Inside that plastic tube is a clear liquid with a little air bubble in it. Now there are two exactly parallel black lines painted on that little tube. When the little bubble in that little tube is exactly between the two lines, you know that whatever you're measuring is perfectly vertical or perfectly horizontal.

If that level is laid on a flat surface, and the bubble is exactly in the middle, you know the surface is in perfect alignment. If the bubble is off center, you know it isn't.

Lots of things look straight and true when you eyeball them from a distance. But it's not until you use the level that you know for certain.

Well, the Bible is God's carpenter's level. If you want to know whether something you are hearing is truth or error, lay the word of God alongside what you are hearing. If it squares with the word of God, if it lines up with the word of God, it's true. If what you hear is out of alignment with God's word, no matter how good it sounds, it's wrong.

As you move toward full manhood in these next years, you will hear a lot of people who will ridicule the Bible and try to convince you it's nothing but superstition and man-made myths. Do not let these people lie to you!

In my freshman year at Stanford University, I had a professor who was responsible for teaching a year-long course on the history of western civilization which all first year students were required to take. It soon became evident that he wanted to use this course to rip to shreds any trace of Christian faith that any student in his class had brought with him to college. He was highly educated, of course, very sophisticated, very persuasive, and utterly contemptuous of Christianity.

The thing that stabilized me that year and kept me from being dragged away from my faith by his snide and snarky lectures was one thing: my confidence that the Bible was and is the word of God, inspired by God and without error. When I laid his view of the world alongside the view of the world I found in the Bible, it just didn't line up anywhere. I made up my mind that I was not going to let anybody move me off the firm stand I had taken on the word of God. In fact, his relentless assault on my faith just ticked me off. It only strengthened my faith and stiffened my resolve. I was not going to let anyone intimidate me or ridicule me into abandoning what I knew was true.

The New Testament says, "All Scripture is breathed out by God" (2 Tim. 3:16a). The word translated "all" in that verse means "any and every." That means no matter where you dip your foot in the pool of God's word, you will be in touch with something that has come from the very soul and mind of God himself.

You can trust it above every human voice you hear. You are building a life, like a carpenter builds a house, one board, one decision at a time. Make sure every decision you make lines up with the Word of God. Like a carpenter's level, it will never let you down.

A Father's Prayer

Father, I pray that you will instill in my son a deep and abiding love and reverence for your word. May he always live with a conviction that your word is right and true and without error. May he come to recognize that your word can always be trusted and is worth more than fine gold. In Jesus' name, amen.

Boys Quit but Men do Not

CHAPTER 9

Boys quit; real men do not.

"For though a righteous man falls seven times, he rises again,
but the wicked are brought down by calamity."
~ Proverbs 24:16 (NIV)

The picture that is painted in this verse is of a man who is running a race and yet continually stumbles and falls. Every time he falls, he is tempted to just lie there, give up, and let the race continue without him. But every time he falls, the righteous man picks himself up, dusts himself off, cleans his wounds, and starts running again with his gaze fixed on the finish line.

Nothing will test your character more as a man than the overwhelming desire to quit. There will be times when you will feel beaten down, rejected, abandoned, and defeated. Everything in you will urge you to give up.

Once in Little League baseball, J.D. came to the plate in the bottom of the last inning with two out and the winning run in scoring position. With the pressure on, he struck out swinging and his team lost the game. He was disappointed, even devastated that he hadn't come through in the clutch and let his teammates down. There were even some tears in the mix.

I felt like the best thing I could do as his dad was take him to Marie Callender's for a piece of his favorite pie. While we were there, we saw part of Ken Burns' documentary on baseball. The program we saw was all about the 1950's, one of the greatest decades in baseball history. It was the decade in which Bobby Thomson hit the "Shot Heard Round the World" to win the pennant for the Giants in 1951. It was the decade in which Willie Mays made perhaps the greatest catch in the history of baseball for the Giants in the 1954 World Series. It was the decade in which Don Larsen pitched the only perfect game in World Series history, for the Yankees in 1956. It was the decade in which Mickey Mantle came to prominence as one of the game's premiere sluggers.

We saw the highlights of all these players in action, and after the program was over, I asked J.D., "You know who my favorite baseball player of all time is?" He said, "No - who?" I said, "I'm looking right at him." He shook off the disappointment of that night's game and kept plugging away.

Boxers have trainers, men who wait for them in their corner of the ring at the end of each round to give them something to drink and a pep talk for the next round. Back in the day, every trainer had a large white towel draped over his shoulder which he used to wipe the sweat and sometimes the blood off his fighter's face.

The towel also was used for one other thing: when the trainer decided his fighter was a beaten man and that it was useless to continue, he'd take the towel off his shoulder and toss it into the ring to let the referee know that he was giving up. That's where we get the expression "to throw in the towel."

God's men don't throw in the towel. No matter how many times they wind up on the canvas, they keep picking themselves up and getting back into the fight.

Life will be full of disappointments and defeats. You won't win every round. You can give something the best you've got, everything you've got, and still lose.

We can't always control the outcome of every fight we have to fight. But the one thing we can control is whether or not we quit. As the saying goes, we can be bloody but unbowed.

Victory in life belongs to the persistent. It belongs to those who hang in there, refuse to throw in the towel, and refuse to quit in discouragement.

A mentor of mine was fond of the expression, "God's men bounce." What he meant by that is a blow that would level a normal man and leave him flat on the floor is a blow that just causes God's man to bounce up off the floor and get back in the battle.

J.D. played baseball in high school. In his junior year, he was the back-up to the starting second baseman. He worked hard at practice, was a faithful and loyal teammate, and prepared himself for the day when he might get his chance to start.

That day came against Timberline, one of the best teams in the state year in and year out. In the fourth inning, the coach sent him in to replace the starting second baseman, who was struggling. Finally, J.D. had his opportunity.

The second batter of the inning hit a blistering ground ball to his left. J.D. bobbled it for an error. The third batter hit a blistering ground ball to his right. J.D. bobbled the back-handed stop for another error. Then the fifth batter of the inning hit a scorching one-hopper right at him, which he fumbled for his third consecutive error of the inning.

The coach replaced him before he had even completed a half-inning of play. That was one of the lowest points of his life, since he not only failed to capitalize on the opportunity but was deeply disappointed that he'd let his teammates down in the process. That was a long night in the Fischer household, I can tell you that. As his father, I would have readily changed places with him to bear his disappointment and hurt. But it was his weight to bear and not mine.

All he could do was to dig deep, trust God, shake off the bad night, refuse to give in to self-pity, and go back out the next day committed to give it everything he had. And that's what he did. He proved himself everyday in practice, dedicated himself to being a good teammate, and eventually he got another opportunity to start, an opportunity he was afraid would never come. And this time he took full advantage of the opportunity, held on to the starting spot, wound up hitting over .300 for the season, and helped his team finish third in the state tournament.

In his senior year, once again he had to fight to win that starting job back. He did, and wound up leading the team in hitting, this time hitting .413. In the first game of the state tournament, he came to the plate with the bases loaded. When he was in the on-deck circle, the assistant coach came over to him, and said, "J.D., I don't want to put any pressure on you, but if you hit one outta here, it's game over."

Well, he turned on a fast ball and crushed it. It soared over the left-center field fence and cleared it by twenty feet. The stands erupted, and J.D. was mobbed by his entire team at the plate. It was a walk-off grand slam. Game over.

I told him after the game, "J.D., the best thing about that home run is that it will be true for the rest of your life." He went on to have a successful career in college, even making an ESPN regional all-academic team and earning some all-conference honors. "For though a righteous man falls seven times, he rises again."

44

Here are the words of Winston Churchill during some of the darkest hours in England's history, when the British were fighting off Nazi Germany virtually alone:

"Never give in. Never give in. Never, never, never, never—in nothing, great or small, large or petty—never give in, except to convictions of honour and good sense. Never yield to force. Never yield to the apparently overwhelming might of the enemy."

Whether it's an academic challenge, an athletic challenge, a romantic disappointment, or a setback in work or career, don't throw in the towel. Wipe the sweat and blood from your brow and get back in the ring. Because boys quit but men do not.

"If you falter in times of trouble, how small is your strength!"
~ Proverbs 24:10 NIV

A FATHER'S PRAYER

Father, I pray that you will develop my son into a man of determination, resolve, and endurance. May you instill in him the character to refuse to give up when he feels like that's all he wants to do. Please grant him the strength and courage to continue to run the race you have set before him with endurance until he has finished his course. In Jesus' name, amen.

Booze and Drugs

CHAPTER 10

Boys abuse drugs and alcohol; real men don't.

"Wine is a mocker, strong drink a brawler, and whoever is led astray by it is not wise." ~ Proverbs 20:1

"Who has woe? Who has sorrow? Who has strife? Who has complaining? Who has wounds without cause? Who has redness of eyes? Those who tarry long over wine...in the end it bites like a serpent and stings like an adder. Your eyes will see strange things, and your heart utter perverse things."
~ Proverbs 23:29-33

As you grow to manhood, you will have a decision to make about the use of both alcohol and drugs.

Many students of Scripture believe that, for adults, drinking alcohol in moderation is permissible according to the Bible, while others believe it is forbidden. The Bible indicates in Romans 14 that this is a matter for each man to decide between himself and God.

But all mature men know that, while drinking itself may not be a sin, drunkenness always is. Lives, marriages, families, and careers have been destroyed by intoxicating beverages that were consumed in excess.

Don't let yourself become another grim statistic. The time is now, right now, to make a decision that you will never get drunk, even if you join a fraternity in college. Young men do really stupid things when they are drunk, including getting into fights ("strong drink [is] a brawler"), and driving under the influence, which can leave them in big trouble or even dead.

And now is the time to decide you will not take drugs, period. The only reason to take any drug, other than one prescribed by your doctor for illness, is to get high. Hard drugs have obvious and destructive effects on males, messing with their minds, their health, their ambitions, and their ability to function.

But even marijuana, which a lot of your peers will call a recreational drug that won't do you any harm, can lead to permanent brain damage. This long-lasting brain damage is particularly pronounced in males who start smoking dope when they are in their teens.

Even casual pot use causes abnormalities in the part of the brain that deals with emotion, motivation, judgment, and planning, meaning pot use will stunt your emotional growth and reduce your drive to succeed in life and your ability to make good decisions.

The earlier someone starts smoking pot, the more the chances are that it will make him slower at tasks, reduce his IQ, and increase his risk of stroke later in life. So if you don't want to be dumber, lazier, sicker, and less successful as an adult, don't even think about lighting up a joint.

Now is the time, right now, to resolve that you will not fry your brain with drugs, even pot. Even a little bit of pot. Just don't do it.

The New Testament is quite direct: "Do not get drunk with wine, for that is debauchery, but be filled with the Spirit" (Eph. 5:18). The word "debauchery" means excessive indulgence in pleasure. What God is warning us about is that when we hand over control of our minds and bodies to substances like drugs or alcohol, it lowers our self-restraint and we wind up doing a lot of things we will live to regret.

We will do things that cannot be undone, all because we were too high or too drunk to make smart choices. Do not let this happen to you.

I took a course in college from a nationally renowned psychologist, Philip Zimbardo. (He directed the infamous "Stanford Prison Experiment" while I was a student there.) He was a leader in his field for a good reason, and was a very entertaining lecturer. For these reasons, his classes were always packed. In this particular class, he devoted one whole class period to hypnotizing the entire class of 400. I watched in amazement as several hundred of my classmates submitted themselves to this, and obediently did everything he instructed them to do, raising their hands in unison, lowering their hands in unison, and writing things in the air with an imaginary pencil.

But I refused to participate in this experiment, for the same reason you should refuse to abuse drugs or alcohol. There was no way in the world I was going to give my mind over to the control of someone or something else for any reason.

The counsel of the Proverbs is this: "Hear, my son, and be wise, and direct your heart in the way. Be not among drunkards...for the drunkard...will come to poverty" (Prov. 23:19-21). The lesson is pretty simple: don't hang with or run with males who like to get drunk and get high. You might even wind up bankrupting yourself and ruining a career for a high that doesn't last.

If you are with friends who start to head down that road, don't go with them. Peel out of there so fast it will give you a nosebleed. You won't regret it.

A Father's Prayer

Father, I pray that you will so fill my son with your Holy Spirit that he will be able to resist every temptation to indulge in drugs or overindulge in alcohol. May he find his joy in you and in his friends and in his family so that he does not need to resort to the artificial happiness that substances bring. Grant him the self-control to resist even the pull of his close friends should they try to pull him off the path you have marked out for him. In Jesus' name, amen.

Anger

CHAPTER 11

**A boy does not know how to control his temper;
a mature man does.**

*"A fool gives full vent to his anger, but a wise man keeps himself
under control." ~ Proverbs 29:11 (NIV)*

There are many things in life that make us angry, and some
of them should. But a man pays careful attention to his anger,
and only expresses it when it's necessary.

A real man is angry at the right things for the right reasons.
A boy, on the other hand, is angry at the wrong things for
the wrong reasons. A real man controls his anger, but anger
controls a boy.

A word or an action done in a flash of anger can destroy
something that has taken years to build. One angry word can
do so much damage to a relationship that it may take years
to get it back to where it was, if you can do it at all. A stick of
dynamite with a short fuse can explode before anybody is at
a safe distance, and it'll send shrapnel everywhere.

Solomon puts it this way: "A hot-tempered man must
pay the penalty" (Prov. 19:19a NIV). There is an unavoid-
able cost an angry man will have to pay. There isn't any way
around it. It can cost a man friendship, a job, a reputation,
and even a career.

All of us blurt out things in anger that we later regret. We
wish we could take those words back, but we can't. The goal we
should strive for, with God's help, is to think before we speak

at all times, but especially when we are angry. Ask yourself this question: will I regret tomorrow what I am about to say or do right now?

"A fool," Solomon says, "shows his annoyance at once" (Prov. 12:16a NIV). The mark of an immature man is that he has a thin skin, is easily angered, and everybody around him knows it. Men like this are no fun to be around. Others are afraid of him, tiptoe around him, and avoid him for their own protection.

"A prudent man overlooks an insult" (Prov. 12:16b NIV.) One mark of maturity is that you don't react negatively to every negative thing that is said about you or to you. You must always have a soft heart but you also must always have a thick skin, so that it takes a whole lot to get you really teed off.

One other problem with anger is that it becomes a gateway for other problems to enter your life. Solomon puts it this way, "Like a city whose walls are broken down is a man who lacks self-control" (Prov. 25:28 NIV).

Cities in Solomon's time depended on strong and sturdy walls to keep their enemies at bay. If the walls were broken down, if there were gaps in the wall, the folks who lived in that city had no protection from the enemies who wanted to destroy them. The enemy could sweep in like a flood.

A man who doesn't exercise self-control has not only opened his soul to the sin of anger, but also to other sins which can come sweeping into his life, sins like pride, defensiveness, bitterness, self-pity, jealousy, and envy. Anger can open doorways to the enemy that can make a mess of your soul.

"Better a patient man than a warrior," says Solomon, "a man who controls his temper than one who takes a city" (Prov. 16:32 NIV). We admire the men in our nation's military who have the courage and skill to defeat our nation's enemies in battle. Solomon says it requires the same kind of strength and willpower to control your temper as it does to be an elite soldier. Overcoming the temptation to let your anger control you rather than the other way round is a huge battle in a man's life, but it is a battle you must win.

A Father's Prayer

Father, I pray that you will produce the fruit of the Spirit of self-control in full measure in my son. May his anger always be under your control so that he will be its master and never its servant. Make him a mighty warrior in your kingdom. In Jesus' name, amen.

Anger, Part II
CHAPTER 12

A boy stirs up dissension; a man makes peace.

"A hot-tempered man stirs up dissension, but a patient man calms a quarrel." ~ Proverbs 15:18 (NIV)

Solomon says, "It is to a man's honor to avoid strife" (Prov. 20:3a NIV). Now as God's men, we're not going to back down - ever - when we need to stand tall for the truth, but neither are we going to go around looking for a fight.

Another problem with a quick temper is that it will drive you to do impulsive and destructive things. A man with an anger problem lashes out at others without thinking. As Solomon says, "A quick-tempered man does foolish things" (Prov. 14:17a NIV), and "a hot-tempered one commits many sins" (Prov. 29:22b NIV).

And if you speak in anger without thinking, people will think less of you because you will have put your immaturity on display. "A quick-tempered man displays folly" (Prov. 14:29b NIV). That is, he puts it out there where everybody can see it.

A man who does not know how to control his anger starts arguments everywhere he goes, but a man who knows how to restrain his own anger can be a calming influence when people around him are getting angrier and angrier and things are getting more and more intense.

This is how Solomon puts it: "A hot-tempered man stirs up dissension, but a patient man calms a quarrel" (Prov. 15:18 NIV).

You also should make a decision right now that you will not hang around with someone who has an anger problem. His influence might rub off on you, and if you are his friend, and you bail him out when his anger gets him in trouble, you'll spend the rest of your friendship trying to save him from himself.

That's why Solomon says, "If you rescue him (a hot-tempered man), you will have to do it again" (Prov. 19:19b NIV). He adds, "Do not make friends with a hot-tempered man, do not associate with one easily angered, or you may learn his ways and get yourself ensnared" (Prov. 22:24-25 NIV). Running with a guy who has a hair-trigger temper is a great way to get yourself into all kinds of trouble.

In contrast, a man of self-control can sow peace instead of discord. People who lived a long time ago knew that oil has a calming effect on the wave action of water as the oil spreads over the water's surface. It's where the expression to "pour oil on troubled waters" comes from. And it doesn't take much oil to do the trick.

Benjamin Franklin once wrote about standing on the edge of a large pond which was being whipped into frothy waves by a strong wind. He poured in just one teaspoonful of oil, and there was an instant calm over several square yards of the pond, "which spread amazingly and extended itself gradually till it reached the lee side, making all that quarter of the pond, perhaps half an acre, as smooth as a looking glass."

You can be that kind of calming influence on others, that kind of peacemaker, a man who knows how to control his temper. By learning to control yourself, you can create an atmosphere of peace and tranquility in your entire sphere of influence. Jesus said, "Blessed are the peacemakers, for they shall be called sons of God" (Matthew 5:9).

A FATHER'S PRAYER:

Father, I pray that you will produce in my son the fruit of the Spirit of self-control that his temper may never get the best of him. And I pray that you will use him to be a calming influence on others when they are angry and agitated. May he be a peacemaker who is known as your son. In Jesus' name, amen.

God Knows Everything About Everything

CHAPTER 13

**Boys sometimes forget that God knows everything;
real men never do.**

*"The eyes of the Lord are in every place, keeping watch on the
evil and the good." ~ Proverbs 15:3*

God knows everything about everything. That means he
knows everything about everybody, and he knows everything about you and me. The word translated "keeping
watch" literally means "to lean forward," emphasizing that
God doesn't miss a thing.

Now this is both good news and bad news. The bad news
is that it means that, in the end, we're not going to get away
with anything. But the good news is that, in the end, no good
thing we ever do goes unnoticed or unrewarded by God.

Satan does not know everything, and he cannot read our
minds either. But God can. Abraham Lincoln is supposed to
have said, "You can fool all the people some of the time, and
some of the people all the time, but you cannot fool all the
people all the time." The biblical sequel to this is that we can't
fool God any of the time.

Solomon says, "Sheol and Abaddon (that's hell) lie open
before the Lord; how much more the hearts of the children of
man!" (Prov. 15:11). God is the only one who can see directly
into hell, and he is also the only one who can see into our
hearts. He knows not just what we do but also what we think.

This means that he's the only one who knows our motives.

We think we do, and sometimes we do. But many times, we don't even know our own hearts well enough to know whether our motives are pure or not.

In fact, we almost always think we're right, even though sometimes we may be wrong. As Solomon says, "All the ways of a man are pure in his own eyes, but the LORD weighs the spirit" (Prov. 16:2). We can and do justify to ourselves almost everything we do.

But God "weighs the spirit," and he may see things there that we miss because we are so busy trying to convince ourselves that we are right and everybody else is wrong.

The spirit is the deepest part of our humanity. And God knows everything that goes on there even though we may not.

I distinctly remember one time saying something strongly to an individual in a group setting. When I said it, I felt absolutely justified in what I had said. But after a while, quite a while actually, my conscience began to trouble me about that one thing I had said. I realized that in reality it was harsh, judgmental, and prideful, and I knew I needed to make things right.

A full eleven years after it had happened I finally sought out that individual to apologize and make things right. Even though it took time for me to see reality, God knew I was wrong the moment I said it, and he spent the next several years getting me to see what he knew all along.

As you grow to manhood, then, it's critical that you grasp the truth that you are not the final judge of whether your motives and behavior are pure. God is.

As Solomon says, "The crucible is for silver, and the furnace is for gold, and the LORD tests hearts" (Prov. 17:3). The way precious metals such as gold and silver were purified back in the day was by applying heat. As the heat rose in the "crucible" or the "furnace," any impurities would rise to the surface where they could be skimmed off.

In the same way, God will often use heat - adversity, disappointment, painful life experiences - to cause the impurities in us to rise to the surface so we can see them and he can remove them. We may wind up seeing things about ourselves we don't like, but that's how we become God's men. It takes high heat to make strong steel.

When silver was refined the old-fashioned way, the refiner would know the job was done when he could see his own reflection in the crucible. And so God will continue to search your heart and do his work of refining and purifying you because he wants his image reflected back to him when he looks at you.

A FATHER'S PRAYER

Heavenly Father, we acknowledge that you and you alone know everything about us. I pray you will continue to search my son's heart, and my heart as well, and bring to the surface any impurities that need to be removed so that we may be your men in every way. In Jesus' name, amen.

Sex

CHAPTER 14

**A mature young man is sexually pure;
an immature young man isn't.**

*"He who finds a wife finds a good thing and obtains favor from
the Lord." ~ Proverbs 18:22*

*"Let your fountain be blessed, and rejoice in the wife of your
youth, a lovely deer, a graceful doe. Let her breasts fill you at
all times with delight (bet you didn't know that verse was in
the Bible did you?); be intoxicated always in her love. Why
should you be intoxicated, my son, with a forbidden woman
and embrace the bosom of an adulteress?" ~ Proverbs 5:18-20*

Why is this woman forbidden to you? For one reason: she's
not your wife.

The time is now, right now, to make up your mind that you
will only have sex with one woman for your entire life. And
that you will wait until you marry her to do it.

Sex is a gift from God. Some people think that God does
not approve of sex, but they're wrong. He approves of it. He
loves it. It's his idea. It is a good thing, a marvelous gift from
our Creator.

It is a powerful force, a force which has the power to bond
two people together in an intimate union that is stronger
than the power of hell itself. It is a powerful expression of
love and commitment and produces an exquisite pleasure
unlike anything else a man can experience.

And by God's design, it is the delightful means by which children are conceived and brought into the world. One of the wonders and delights that await you is the privilege of raising children together with your wife, knowing that those children are the fruit of your love for each other. There is nothing like that satisfaction in all the world.

But because sex is such a powerful force, it must be used wisely and with restraint, because it has the power to destroy as well as to build up. It must be channeled exclusively into the relationship a man has with his wife. Used outside marriage, it can ruin a man's whole life and turn it into rubble.

Now the world won't tell you this. It will try to tell you that sex before marriage or outside marriage is exhilarating, exciting, and problem-free. The world and anyone in it who tries to tell you that is wrong. Dead wrong.

There is probably no single thing that has done more damage to human society than sex either before or outside of marriage. Sexually transmitted diseases, children born out of wedlock, and broken hearts are all part of the bitter legacy of sexual immorality. Now, right now, is the time to decide that you will not fall into that trap.

Here's the way Solomon puts it in Proverbs 7, looking at a young man who did not have the smarts to draw clear boundaries around his own sexuality:

"I have perceived among the youths, a young man lacking sense, passing along the street near her corner, taking the road to her house in the twilight, in the evening, at the time of night and darkness" (Prov. 7:7-9).

J.D. and Bryan
Here I am, planning ahead - getting him used to mowing my lawn.

J.D., Bryan and Matt
J.D. and his best buddy Matt teaching me to read.

J.D. and Bryan
Rocking our red satin jackets.

J.D. and Bryan
Getting ready to go deep under the watchful eye of his first coach.

Bryan and J.D.
Getting his baseball career started in Little League.

Bryan and J.D.
Watching a Giants game in the Old Candlestick Park - Barry Bonds hit the year's longest home run in this game.

Bryan and J.D.
J.D. as a senior at Whitman College - earned all-conference honors and a place
on ESPN's All-Academic team for his region.

J.D. and Bryan

Just hanging at some amusement park somewhere.

AT&T Park

Message board at AT&T park on our anniversary, courtesy of J.D. - Message: "Way to lock down that gamer babe, Dad!"

Bryan and J.D.
Rocking our Giants' game jerseys at AT&T Park on our 40th anniversary trip.

Sarah and J.D.
I had the privilege and honor of performing the wedding ceremony for J.D. and his beautiful bride Sarah.

This young man made a profound mistake you must learn to avoid: he put himself in a position where he was likely to be tempted. It can be in the backseat of your car, in her parents' house when they're away for the evening or out of town, at a frat party in college, at an office party, or on a business trip when you might think about having a nightcap at the hotel bar before you turn in.

It doesn't matter. The smart thing for you to do is to stay out of risky situations altogether. You might even be drawn to a situation, as this young man was, perhaps secretly hoping that the situation you are heading into might just lead in some way to a sexual encounter.

"Behold, the woman meets him, dressed as a prostitute, wily of heart. She is loud and wayward...now in the street, now in the market, and at every corner she lies in wait" (Prov. 7:10-12).

The simplest way to put it is that you can know exactly which women to avoid by the way they dress. If a woman is dressed in a sexually seductive or suggestive way - whether at school, at college, at the office, or even at church - your mission is to avoid her like she was a carrier of the bubonic plague. Because from a moral standpoint she is.

Solomon's young man wasn't smart enough to do that. Solomon goes on:

"She seizes him and kisses him, and with bold face says to him,...'I have come out to meet you, to seek you eagerly, and I have found you. I have spread my couch with coverings, colored linens from Egyptian linen; I have perfumed my bed with myrrh, aloes, and cinnamon. Come, let us take our fill of love

till morning; let us delight ourselves with love. For my husband is not at home'...With much seductive speech she persuades him; with her smooth talk she compels him" (Proverbs 7:13-21).

Such a woman may initiate a sexual encounter, may tell you how attractive you are, and might even blow smoke up your nose by telling you that you are just the one she's been looking for. Don't believe her. Run, run like the wind.

I remember once, in junior high school no less, being approached by a female classmate who exuded sexual availability. Her reputation had preceded her, and she'd already acquired a well-deserved notoriety on campus. She had now turned her attentions to me and indicated clearly that she was available if I was.

I made it a point from that moment on to avoid her in any and every way possible. I made it a point never to be alone with her anywhere at any time, and never had another conversation with her until we both graduated high school and went separate ways.

Debbie and I and our two kids went skiing one weekend. They were up in the lodge while I went for my last run of the day. It was a busy day at this ski resort, so they wanted two people in every chair on the lift. So if you were skiing solo, as I was, you were supposed to holler out "Single!" as you approached the lift so that anyone else in line who was also skiing solo could ride with you.

As I approached the lift I did as instructed and hollered, "Single!" as I turned back to see if anyone needed a lift. A very attractive young woman waved, skied over, batted her eyes, and invitingly said, "I'm a single single!" It didn't take a rocket surgeon to figure out she was signaling availability.

I smiled in return, and said quite firmly, "Well, I'm a married single!" As we got on the lift, I began immediately talking about my wife and my family up in the lodge, to signal clearly to her that I was off limits. We had a pleasant chat on the ride up, and I never saw her again.

My son used to worry his mom to death when we went camping back in the day. We'd always build a ring around our campfire out of rocks. But J.D. found the fire fascinating and irresistible and would get as close to the fire as he could without falling in. Debbie was always afraid he at some point was going to trip over the rocks and land right on his keister in the middle of the flames. (Fortunately, this never happened.)

Now Solomon's young man knew he was dancing too close to the fire of sexual temptation. He knew that what he was thinking about doing was wrong. But because he toyed with sexual immorality, tried to get as close to the blaze as he could without being burned, he eventually fell into the fire. He resisted temptation for a time, then his will and resistance collapsed.

"All at once he follows her, as an ox goes to the slaughter, or as a stag is caught fast till an arrow pierces his liver...he does not know that it will cost him his life" (Prov. 7:22-23).

His problem began way before the sexual encounter began. His problem began when he turned down her street. Protecting your sexual purity will require decisions that physically keep you from even entering into situations where you may be tempted to the breaking point.

When Debbie and I were dating, she lived by herself in her own apartment. To protect the purity of our relationship, we saved our expressions of physical affection for the door as I was on my way out. Because I am 15 inches taller than she is, I even built a little kissing stand which we parked by the door. Deb would step up on that stand and that's where we'd exchange a good night kiss and a good night hug just before I left.

Working my way through college, I worked one summer in a slaughterhouse. My job was to run cattle from the holding pen up into what was called the kill chute. I'd run five cattle at a time up this ramp, and then drop a door behind the last one so they could not back down the ramp even if they wanted to.

The cattle would be ushered one by one into the actual kill chute, a box with room for just one animal at a time. Then we would knock them unconscious with a thing called a knocker. We'd tap the trigger, which was at the end of something that looked like an axe handle, on the top of the head of the unsuspecting animal. The trigger would fire off a .22 shell, which would drive a plunger into the animal's skull, fracturing it and rendering the animal unconscious. Then we'd pull a lever, a side door to the kill chute would open, and the animal would roll down onto the kill floor, where it would be strung up by its rear hooves and its throat slit. It would die as its lifeblood drained away. The poor beast never knew what hit him.

Why do I describe this scenario in such graphic detail? Because, my young friend, you are that animal if you do not flee sexual temptation.

Now no man other than Jesus has handled his sexuality perfectly; he went to the cross to provide forgiveness for every sin, including our sexual sin. But the standard is clear, and by God's grace, you can meet it.

A Father's Prayer

Father, I pray that you will cause a powerful spirit of sexual purity, self-control, and wisdom to rest upon my son. Please teach him to flee sexual immorality and to do everything in his power to avoid it. By your grace, power, and mercy, may he be able to reserve his sexual energy for his wife alone. In Jesus' name, amen.

Pornography

CHAPTER 15

**A mature young man avoids pornography;
an immature young man doesn't.**

*"I made a covenant with my eyes not to look lustfully at a
young woman." ~ Job 31:1 (NIV)*

*"I will set no worthless thing before my eyes...it shall not fasten
its grip on me." ~ Psalm 101:3 (NASB)*

Pornography - pictures or videos of naked people having
sex - is everywhere. It's just a click away on virtually any
electronic device.

Social research indicates that most young boys your age
have been exposed to pornography. In fact, the average age of
a boy when he is first exposed to porn is now down to about
10, and it will likely continue to drop.

Porn is everywhere because males are sexual beings. We
are designed in such a way that we will respond to sexual
stimuli, including of the visual kind. Any normal male
exposed to pornography will feel the pull of it. I was exposed
to pornography as a young teen, and I know how enticing it
can be. Now feeling that draw to porn is not something by
itself to be ashamed of - that's a normal reaction based on the
way we are made.

But as understandable as the attraction is, you must learn
to resist its pull. While the draw to it is understandable, you
must learn to refuse to yield to that pull. You must learn to

resist the temptation to indulge in pornography. The reason is simple: if you consume pornography, it will consume you in the end.

Addiction to pornography is a terrible thing. And it can start at a very young age. In Britain, researchers have discovered that about 25% of all the young boys around the age of 12 who have been put in facilities to get intense psychological counseling are there because they have become addicted to porn. It results in terrible feelings of guilt - because we know it's wrong -, isolation, depression, and even self-hatred. Don't let this happen to you.

There are many reasons to avoid pornography beyond the guilt and the isolation it causes. It will harm the way you look at females, and lead you to think of them primarily as sex objects rather than as individuals made in the image of God.

It will distort your view of sex. Sex is designed by God to be something warm and tender between a man and his wife, which is never how pornographic sex is portrayed.

It may even harm your ability to engage in sexual intimacy with your wife. Even young men in the peak of physical health who get addicted to porn discover that it can cripple their ability even to function sexually with their wives.

The time to make up your mind about porn is now. "Why," the Bible says, "should you be intoxicated, my son, with a forbidden woman?" (Proverbs 5:20a).

Now if you do succumb to temptation, remember that God is always available to forgive you just as soon as you confess your sin to him and claim his forgiveness. Don't try to hide your sin from him, because he sees everything. Instead, bring it out into the open before him and honestly admit your sin to him. "If we confess our sins, he is faithful and just to forgive us our sins and to cleanse us from all unrighteousness" (1 John 1:9). Don't hesitate to claim that promise of God as often as you need to.

If you feel yourself getting sucked in, you may have to realize you may not be able to overcome porn by yourself. You may need to share your struggle with a good friend or even better with your father and ask him to pray for you.

As a pastor, I counseled men who had fallen into an addiction to porn. In some cases, they even lost their jobs when they were busted using porn at work. The only way out for them was to find a trusted friend who would hold them accountable and pray for them on a weekly basis.

The New Testament says, "confess your sins to one another and pray for one another, that you may be healed" (James 5:16). The men who followed this biblical counsel experienced victory over pornography. Not always immediately or dramatically, but by sticking with accountability and prayer, they got themselves free with God's help.

Somebody once compared consuming porn to drinking water from a toilet. As we talked about before, God's will for you is to wait for sexual expression until you can enjoy it with the woman of God's choice for you. The Bible uses the imagery of drinking fresh, pure water to describe engaging in sexual intimacy with your wife. "Drink water from your own cistern, flowing water from your own well...Let your fountain be blessed, and rejoice in the wife of your youth." (Prov. 5:15, 18). It will be worth the wait.

A Father's Prayer

Father, I pray for my son. I pray that you will fill him with a powerful spirit of self-control, patience, and sexual purity.

Please free him from all forms of sexual immorality, including pornography. I pray that by your grace and mercy he will be able to wait for that day when you bring the woman of your choice into his life. In Jesus' name I pray, amen.

Dating

CHAPTER 16

A mature man only courts a woman who loves God more than she loves him.

As you continue on the glide path toward mature manhood, the day will soon come when you will want to pursue a relationship with a girl who grabs your attention. You'll be entering into the dating or courtship phase of your life.

These are perilous waters, and you want to navigate them in such a way that you can look back on these days without regret.

How do you do that? Number one, accept the parameters established by your father as long as you are living at home. Every father will have slightly different standards than other dads. That's fine. Your job is not to compare your dad's standards to anyone else's. It's to honor your father by accepting his standards and following them.

These standards will have to do with such things as whether your dad follows the courtship model or the more conventional dating model. His standards will deal with issues such as when you can start going on group dates, when you can start going on solo dates (in our house it was group stuff only until 16, then solo dates with permission and strict curfews til graduation), where you can go, and when you have to be back. The day will come when you'll be out having fun and want your dad to extend curfew. Well, call him, make your case, and then do what he says.

Regardless of the approach your father takes, accept his guidance and follow his lead. He loves you more than any other father does. So follow his guidelines. Your father knows that the day will come when you will be on your own, away at college for instance, and will be in a position where you will have to make choices on your own. He's got you on a glide path to prepare you for that day.

What about whom you date? When we talk about marriage, we'll establish a principle: don't marry anyone who doesn't love God more than she loves you. It's the same in dating. Dating, or courtship, is the process by which you seek a mate for life. It's a process that should in the end lead you to the woman with whom you will spend the rest of your life.

That's its ultimate purpose. So your desires for a lifelong mate should guide your dating and courtship decisions.

I remember a dating seminar in college, where our campus pastor used the analogy of being unequally yoked together. That's a metaphor from the world of agriculture, in which two animals were put in the same harness to work a field together. Yoking two animals of different kinds just didn't work because of differences in size, gait, and strength. You'd never, for instance, yoke an ox and a camel together. It would wind up being cruel and unfair to both.

So our mentor advised us against marrying anyone who didn't share our deepest spiritual values. To do so would be to go through life unequally yoked which will wind up being bad for everybody. So naturally one of the guys raised his hand and asked, "Is it okay to date a camel as long as you don't marry one?" Everybody laughed, but it was a good question. And the best answer is "No."

My advice to you is don't even date someone who doesn't love God with her whole heart, soul, strength and mind. That ought to be a non-negotiable standard in dating as well as in marriage. You may have fewer dates that way, but trust me, you will also have fewer regrets.

A Father's Prayer

Father, I pray that you will protect my son's heart. Grant him wisdom as he seeks a mate, that he will be prompted by you to seek a mate who loves you more even than she loves him. May his standards in dating and courtship be the same as yours in every respect. In Jesus' name, amen.

Dating: How Far Can You Go?

CHAPTER 17

A mature young man always treats his dates with honor; a boy doesn't.

When you start dating, you should always remember that the chances are pretty good you are not going to marry the girl you happen to be dating at the moment. One of the things I told my son: this means you are dating a girl who one day is going to be another man's wife. Treat her accordingly.

The corollary is that somebody else right now may be dating the woman who one day will be your wife. How do you want him to treat her? That's how you should treat every girl you date. Don't do anything with her that you would not want the guy who right now is dating your future wife to do with her.

As far as physical involvement in dating is concerned, I believe there is one rule you need to remember. Now I went to seminars when I was in college where we got advice about where our hands could go, what kind of kissing was allowed, and what kind of physical expression was permitted. It all got pretty complicated. There's a better and simpler way.

Back in the day, the United States had what we called the Distant Early Warning System. It was a radar system designed to alert us to a Russian military launch over the North Pole. It was for our protection so we could stop bad things from happening before it was too late.

As a mentor of mine pointed out to me when I was single, God has given to young men an absolutely infallible warning system that lets a guy know without fail when it's time to stop.

That infallible biological signal is sexual arousal.

As soon as you find yourself becoming sexually aroused - experiencing an erection -, you need to stop whatever it is you're doing, even if it's just holding hands, to keep things from escalating. And make up your mind that you won't do whatever that thing is again until you get married.

When a dating couple gets sexually involved, their relationship instantly stops developing and growing. Sexual involvement will freeze that relationship right where it is, and it will never grow beyond that point. But when sexual energy is reserved for marriage, physical intimacy becomes a dynamic part of a growing and maturing relationship.

Bottom line: some things are worth waiting for, and saving sex for marriage is one of those things.

A Father's Prayer

Father, I pray that you will cause a strong spirit of sexual purity to rest on my son as he moves through this stage in his life. Grant him great wisdom in pursuing relationships with young women. May he always treat them with honor and protect their sexual purity. Lead him, in your time, to the woman of your choice for him. In Jesus' name, amen.

Finding a Wife

CHAPTER 18

**A real man chooses a wife based on character;
a boy chooses a wife based on looks.**

*"He who finds a wife finds a good thing and obtains favor from
the Lord." ~ Proverbs 18:22*

*"An excellent wife who can find? She is far more precious than
jewels." ~ Proverbs 31:10*

The most important decision you will ever make in your
life is what you do with God.

The second most important decision you will ever make is
your choice of a wife.

Solomon talks here about "finding" a wife. Now there are two
ways to find something: by accident or on purpose. Solomon
is talking about searching for the right woman to marry
until you find her. He's talking about being intentional and
purposeful in seeking a mate. That's a decision that's way too
important to be left to chance. Great marriages don't just
happen; they are built by design.

So how do you find the right woman to marry?

First, ask God for his help. Solomon says, "A prudent wife
is from the Lord" (Prov. 19:14b). God wants you to find the
right wife even more than you do. Trust him to lead you to
the right woman, and constantly ask for his counsel and guidance in all your relationships. He knows everything about ev-

erything, so he will see things that you don't. Ask him to show you everything you need to know to make a good choice.

Seek counsel from your father and your mother, and seek counsel from your friends. Ask them to be honest with you. They love you enough to want you to make a good choice in a mate almost as much as you do; in fact, your parents want you to make a good choice even more than you do. Sometimes they will see things that you might miss because love truly is blind. Be very reluctant to move forward in a relationship without the support of those closest to you, and especially without the blessing of your dad and your mom.

Second, only marry a woman who loves God more than she loves you. In fact, don't even date a woman who does not love God more than she loves you. Why is this important? Because there will be times in your marriage where you may not even like her very much, and she may not be very happy with you. What will get you through the rough patches in marriage is your commitment to God and the commitment your wife has made not only to you but to God.

Debbie and I took the word "divorce" out of our marriage vocabulary altogether. It was simply not an option that was ever on the table. That meant that we had to find a way to work through the difficult times because ending the relationship was not an option. I used to joke with people, "Debbie and I have never considered divorce. Homicide, maybe, but never divorce!"

Third, don't be in a hurry. The father of a college friend of mine told his son, "Go slow and get to know." Get to know the woman you're dating well enough to get past the surface stuff and the infatuation to get an accurate picture of her character and her soul, what she's really like under the makeup.

Fourth, don't base your selection on looks, as tempting as that might be. Solomon says, "Like a gold ring in a pig's snout is a beautiful woman without discretion" (Prov. 11:22). Outer beauty on a woman without inner character is about as attractive as expensive jewelry on a wild hog.

A guy I knew in college had a father who always told him, "Beauty is skin deep, but ugly goes right to the bone." There's a long list of men who wind up unhappily married because they chose a wife simply for her looks with no consideration of her character.

Solomon puts it this way: "Charm is deceitful, and beauty is vain, but a woman who fears the Lord is to be praised" (Prov. 31:30).

Solomon adds, "An excellent wife is the crown of her husband, but she who brings shame is like rottenness in his bones" (Prov. 12:4). A good wife can make a man look good and bring public credit and honor to him - she can be his "crown" - or she can be a woman who embarrasses him.

"A quarrelsome wife is like a constant dripping" (Prov. 19:13b NIV). Now disagreements and arguments in marriage are inevitable but a woman who is constantly picking fights and is argumentative is not a woman you want to marry. In fact, Solomon says it is better to "live in a desert" or "in the corner of the roof" than "with a quarrelsome and ill-tempered wife" (Prov. 21:9, 19 NIV).

Read Proverbs 31:10-31 sometime. It tells you to look for a woman who is not lazy but willing to work hard, a woman who makes good decisions, who has compassion for others, a good sense of humor, strength of character, and is a woman whose "children rise up and call her blessed" (Prov. 31:28).

How to identify such a woman? The last phrase used in

the previous paragraph leads to the key question. What kind of mother will she make? This question cuts through all the surface stuff and gets right to the issue of heart and character. The single most important question to ask yourself is this: Do I want this woman to be the mother of my children? When the answer to that question is "yes," you've found the woman for you.

That's how I recognized Debbie as the woman I wanted to marry, and she has been everything I could have hoped for as a friend, partner, companion, and mother to my children. I would happily marry her all over again.

Debbie and I celebrated our 40th anniversary not too long ago. To make it a true celebration, I took Debbie and our grown kids and their spouses on a long weekend trip to San Francisco, where Debbie and I had spent our honeymoon. We stayed in Sausalito, a quaint little town just north of San Francisco, in a house with a spectacular view of the bay and the San Francisco skyline.

We rode the ferry over to the the City by the Bay every day, gliding past the Golden Gate Bridge and Alcatraz as the skyline came into view. We had breakfast at the historic Buena Vista Cafe, bought San Francisco Giants gear at Fisherman's Wharf, drove over to the beach for a day, walked through the Muir Redwoods, and took in two Giants' games.

(One night we watched a movie called "San Andreas," which is about an earthquake that basically destroys all of San Francisco. Not everything about the weekend was romantic.)

When our friends heard about the Giants' games, they expressed their sympathy for Deb. "Why, that man is dragging that poor woman to baseball games on their anniversary!" In truth, Debbie dragged me to the games. (Not that I minded, you understand.) She loves baseball, in part because we spent years following J.D. all over the Northwest to watch him play in high school and college, and it got in her blood.

And also we had gone to a Giants' game on our honeymoon and again on our 10th anniversary, so it had become something of a family tradition.

At the first game, we discovered that J.D. had arranged ahead of time to have the Giants put a giant "Happy 40th Anniversary" message to Debbie and me on the Jumbotron, with a message at the bottom that said, "Way to lock down that gamer babe, Dad!"

For our anniversary dinner, I took us all to a romantic restaurant in Sausalito built out over the waters of the bay, with the lights of San Francisco in clear view. The backstory here is that I never properly proposed to Debbie when we got engaged, and didn't even have a ring for her. Well, this time was going to be different.

Early that year, I snuck the engagement ring that Debbie's Mom had received from her Dad out of her jewelry armoire. There was hardly anything left of it. Most of the ring was gone, as well as the stones. There wasn't much left other than the setting. I had a jeweler rebuild it, pretty much from scratch, with new diamonds and new rubies, and she did a spectacular job.

After dinner was over, I pushed the table at which Debbie and I had been sitting out of the way, and got down on my knees, which she didn't see coming. I confess I got all choked up (must have been some dust in the air). I told her the same thing I had said to her when we got engaged originally, borrowing a line from an old Jim Croce song (it wasn't old when we got engaged!)

Through my tears, I said, "Babe, I love you so much and I'm so glad I am married to you. And I want you to know that I've looked around long enough to know that you are STILL the one I want to go through time with." Then I extended the ring to her and said, "Would you be willing to marry me all over again?" She said "Yes." When I slipped the ring on her finger, the entire section of the restaurant in which we were sitting cheered and clapped.

Marry wisely and one day you will be able to say the same thing to your bride.

A Father's Prayer

Father, I pray that you will bring the woman of your choice into my son's life when the time is right. Please grant him the wisdom to recognize her when that time comes. Protect him from his own folly in his choice of a mate. Please bless him and lead him to a woman who will be his lifelong companion and best friend. Please lead him to a woman with whom he can build a beautiful family. In Jesus' name, amen.

Work

CHAPTER 19

A man works hard; a boy is a slacker.

"All hard work brings a profit, but mere talk leads on to poverty." ~ Proverbs 14:23 (NIV)

"Lazy hands make a man poor, but diligent hands bring wealth." ~ Proverbs 10:4 (NIV)

As a man, God has made you for work. Working hard with your own hands to provide for your needs and the needs of your family is central to what it means to be a man. You have been called to be both a protector and a provider for your family.

One of my good friends is independently wealthy, and did not need to work a single day in his life. (To his credit, he developed a successful career as a pastor and then a counselor, refusing to coast on inherited wealth.) I wasn't in his position. If I didn't work, my family didn't eat.

I've never regretted that, even for a single day, and never wished I could have traded places with him. I found great satisfaction in knowing that my wife and my children were depending on me, and that I was taking care of them. "The laborer's appetite works for him; his hunger drives him on" (Prov. 16:26, NIV). I like to eat, and I wanted my family to be able to eat, and that drove me to work hard.

In fact, I'd urge you not even to think about retiring down the road. Sure, you may reach a point where you can slow down, and may shift your energies to a different kind of work. For instance, I have a good friend who "retired" from a long and successful career with a high tech firm, but soon found himself working as an administrator in his local church. As men, God made us to engage in productive work as long as God gives us breath. As I used to tell the men in my church, don't retire, reload.

Some people wrongly think that work is a consequence of sin, but that's not what the Bible teaches. God placed man in the garden of Eden "to work it and to keep it" (Gen. 2:16), well before sin entered the human race.

Now to be sure, sin has made work more difficult than God intended it to be. Because of Adam's sin, God said, "Cursed is the ground because of you; in pain you shall eat of it all the days of your life; thorns and thistles it shall bring forth for you...by the sweat of your face you shall eat bread" (Gen. 3:17-19).

Notice the promise God has made to us here. Even though work will be tiring and frustrating at times, nevertheless God assures you that through your hard work "you shall eat."

There is no job that is free of "thorns and thistles," little things that keep a good job from being a perfect job. I was talking with a friend of mine once, back in the 1980s, before the era of computers had arrived. He was an insurance adjuster, and he loved every part of his work except for one thing: his employer insisted that every form he turned in had to be filled out in triplicate, meaning he had to turn in three copies of every form.

In those days, he had to use a typewriter and carbon paper, which had ink that kept getting all over his hands. It was a perfect job, except for that one little thing, and it aggravated him no end. Every job you ever have will have its thorns and thistles, its carbon paper, but my friend worked hard at his job and it enabled him to support himself and his family.

And so it will be for you. Your thorns and thistles may be difficult bosses, difficult co-workers, and maybe even forms you have to fill out. The point is that even a good job is not going to be a perfect job. But stick with it, power through it, and you will learn what Solomon teaches: "The plans of the diligent lead surely to abundance, but everyone who is hasty comes only to poverty" (Prov. 21:5).

Your first job will be doing chores for your folks. Your dad will be your first boss. Learn how to take correction from him and make it your aim to please him by doing your chores faithfully and well. You'll begin to develop work habits - discipline, responsibility, being a self-starter, meeting deadlines, and working without grumbling - that you will need in the workplace for the rest of your life.

Never think that any job is beneath you. Remember that there is nobility and "profit" in "all hard work." On my glide path to developing my career, I worked in a car wash (making $1.65 an hour), a slaughterhouse, a tomato packing shed, a vineyard picking grapes, a department store, a steel and wire factory, in more than one restaurant as a waiter, and for a company that turned grapes into raisins.

I also worked as a radio disc jockey, a sports broadcaster doing local high school football and basketball games, and for ABC television working in the production truck for baseball broadcasts from the old Astrodome in Houston and football broadcasts from Cowboys Stadium in Dallas. I learned something valuable in every job.

Do not make it your aim to get rich. Some guys so devote

themselves to their work, to getting ahead, to piling up a fortune, that they lose everything that matters to them. Always place your confidence in God, never in money. Money can be here today and gone tomorrow, through circumstances that are beyond our control. Solomon warns, "Do not wear yourself out to get rich; have the wisdom to show restraint. Cast but a glance at riches, and they are gone, for they will surely sprout wings and fly off to the sky like an eagle" (Prov. 23:4-5, NIV).

A good friend of mine, who was in a Bible study fellowship group with me, was a very good stock broker. On October 29, 1987, a day now known as Black Monday, the stock market took its biggest drop in history. My friend lost a large percentage of his wealth on a single day. He didn't know how to handle it, and eventually on a bleak New Year's Day, he went out into a field near his palatial home and killed himself. He had placed his hope in money rather than God, and his riches had sprouted wings and flown off like an eagle.

A mentor of mine in graduate school told us one day that he'd talked to a lot of prosperous men toward the end of their lives. He said, "I've had a lot of them tell me their biggest regret is they spent too much time at the office. I've never had a single one of them tell me his biggest regret was that he spent too much time with his family."

I've never made a lot of money. My income, almost from the first day of my working life, has been just about right at or even a little below the median income level for the country. That meant that half the people in America made more than I did, and half made less. I've never made enough money to get rich, but God has always supplied our needs and we have been quite content.

So you are to work hard, but you must keep your life in balance. Invest in your family; you'll never regret it. Besides, no man ever got shot doing the dishes or changing a diaper. Happy wife, happy life. You will discover at the end of your life that the only two things that really matter are God and your family. If you can get that figured out right now and never forget it, you'll be way ahead of the game.

We are not to wear ourselves out to get rich, but on the other hand, are we not to be lazy either. Solomon has much to say about what he calls a "sluggard," someone who is simply too lazy to work hard. A sluggard always has an excuse as to why he can't get to work or apply for a job. "There is a lion outside!" he says, "I shall be killed in the streets!" (Prov. 22:13).

Solomon pictures a sluggard like a man who has a bowl of M&Ms in his lap and falls asleep with his hand still buried in the candy. "The sluggard buries his hand in the dish; he is too lazy to bring it back to his mouth" (Prov. 26:15, NIV). Quite an image, isn't it?

At another point, Solomon pictures the slacker as a guy who is just too lazy to get out of bed to go to work. Instead, he simply rolls over when the alarm goes off. "As a door turns on its hinges, so does a sluggard on his bed" (Prov. 26:14). That's another vivid word picture. Instead of getting up, he just turns over on his side, like a door opening and then closing, back and forth, while the day marches on.

The lesson? "A little sleep, a little slumber, a little folding of the hands to rest - and poverty will come on you like a bandit" (Prov. 24:33-34 NIV). Solomon's point? Don't be that guy.

"Two things I ask of you, O LORD; do not refuse me before I die; Keep falsehood and lies far from me; give me neither poverty nor riches, but give me only my daily bread.Otherwise, I may have too much and disown you and say, 'Who is the LORD?' Or I may become poor and steal, and so dishonor the name of my God." ~ Proverbs 30:7-9, (NIV)

A FATHER'S PRAYER

Father, I pray that you will grow my son into a man who works hard to supply his own needs and the needs of his family. Please direct him to a career and a line of work that will make full use of all the abilities and talents you have given to him. And bless the labor of his hands that his needs may be abundantly satisfied. In Jesus' name, amen.

Money

CHAPTER 20

A real man is smart with his money; a boy isn't.

As you get older, people will start dangling get-rich-quick schemes in front of you that promise instant wealth with little to no work. Make up your mind you will avoid all such quick-strike schemes, for the simple reason that they don't work and you may lose every dime you've invested. "He who works his land will have abundant food, but the one who chases fantasies (i.e., shortcuts to making big money) will have his fill of poverty" (Prov. 28:19, NIV).

A prominent Christian businessman in my hometown, a friend of mine, once promised his fellow Christians that if they invested their money with his business, they would receive an interest rate of two percentage points above prime, that is, two percentage points above the best return they could get anywhere else. Because of his prominence in the Christian community, dozens if not hundreds of churchgoers took the plunge.

It sounded too good to be true, because it was. What he was doing was illegal. He wound up in a federal penitentiary and his investors lost everything. They had all chased a fantasy and wound up with their fill of poverty.

Many years ago, I developed a good friendship with an affluent man, a developer. We met one day for coffee. He pulled up to the coffee shop in a brand new Mercedes, all leather interior, tricked out with the latest in automotive accessories at the time, such as a state of the art stereo system. I pulled up in an old, beat-up, pale green 1966 Volkswagen Beetle, with no state-of-the art anything. (The only thing it had was my favorite all time bumper sticker, the only bumper sticker I've ever put on a car: "Be alert. We need more lerts.")

My friend shared with me that he was in a desperate place. It turns out he owed more to the IRS than I will make in my entire life. I drove away feeling sorrow for my friend but without a twinge of envy for his lifestyle, his home, his cars, or his country club membership. "Whoever trusts in his riches will fall, but the righteous will flourish like a green leaf" (Prov. 11:28). I couldn't wait to get home to our tiny little house (all 960 square feet of it), my lovely bride, and our two beautiful children.

My friend, sadly, went through a traumatic divorce, a traumatic bankruptcy, and eventually committed suicide. It truly is better to be poor and happy than rich and miserable. (One guy said, "Why does it have to be either-or? Why can't I be moderately wealthy and just a little moody?") As Solomon says, "Better a little with the fear of the LORD, than great wealth with turmoil. Better a meal of vegetables where there is love than a fattened calf (think juicy New York strip steak here) with hatred" (Prov. 15:16-17, NIV).

The key to providing financially for your future is to have a good plan and stick with it. I'd urge you to think about what I call the "10-10-80" plan. Give to God's kingdom 10% of what you make right off the top, save another 10% (15% if you can), and live on the rest. Start doing this with your allowance and your very first paycheck. The savings might not seem like much at first, but in time it will grow. For instance, if you invest just $300 a month staring at age 21, you'll be a millionaire by the time you're 65. Solomon says,

"He who gathers money little by little makes it grow" (Prov. 13:11b, NIV).

Think about setting a little bit aside every month just to give away. That way, you're ready to respond to someone else's need on a moment's notice. The most fun Debbie and I have is giving anonymous gifts to those around us who are in a bit of a jam.

God will reward your generosity to him and to others. "A generous man will prosper;

he who refreshes others will himself be refreshed" (Prov. 11:25, NIV). If you give faithfully to God, you will be amazed at his supply. You'll get to the end of a year, look back at your income compared to your expenses, and wonder, "How in the world did we make it?" You made it because God honors his word.

Some people decide they cannot afford to give to God right now, but they'll get around to it one day. But shortchanging God is the quickest route to becoming financially strapped. "One man gives freely, yet gains even more; another withholds unduly, but comes to poverty" (Proverbs 11:24, NIV).

Avoid debt like the plague. If you go to college, student debt is an enormous trap. Keep your student debt to an absolute minimum. I made it through college with a combination of scholarships, help from my parents, summer jobs, and working during the school year as a hasher in my fraternity and as a fireman in the campus fire department. I graduated with just $200 in student debt.

Keep the number of your credit cards to an absolute minimum and pay off the balance every month. Think about saving up and buying used cars for cash. (We've never purchased a new car; after all, as soon as you drive it off the lot, it's a used car.) Don't buy more house than you can afford, and pay off your mortgage as soon as you can. You can pay off a 30-year mortgage in just 21 years by making one extra house payment a year that you apply directly to the principal on your loan.

Once you get out of debt, stay out of debt. Debbie and I have worked very hard to get to the place where we are debt-free. Our house is paid for, our cars are paid for, and we have a zero balance on our credit cards. And we have a lot of peace of mind to boot.

Your best bet is to keep yourself from getting into debt from day one. If you don't, and allow yourself to slide into increasing debt, that debt will hover over your head like a dark rain cloud. There's no fun and a lot of anxiety in owing money to people you can't pay. Truly Solomon was right when he said, "The borrower is the slave of the lender" (Prov. 22:7).

Handle all your financial dealings, whether personal or business, with absolute honesty and integrity. Back in Solomon's day, vendors often did business with a pair of scales and a set of weights. When a customer wanted to buy something, what he wanted to purchase was put in one pan of the scales, and the vendor would put weights from his bag in the other pan until the scales balanced.

He would then charge the customer based on the weight of his purchase, a lot like what we do with fresh vegetables today at the grocery store. The quickest way to cheat a customer was to carry false weights in your bag. Instead of having a one pound weight in your bag, for instance, you might have one that weighed 17 ounces and another which weighed 15 ounces. You'd use whichever one would be to your advantage. For example, the customer might think he was buying a pound of something when in reality he was only buying 15 ounces worth. Because of the similarity in size and weight, customers couldn't tell they were being ripped off.

God absolutely detests this way of doing business. "A false balance is an abomination to the Lord, but a just weight is his delight" (Prov. 11:1). Don't cheat in business, ever, and don't take what does not belong to you, whether in something great or small. Debbie and I were out to dinner once, when the waiter, without realizing it, gave me too much change in return. I pointed it out to him, and gave him back what was rightfully his. He was amazed, and thanked me profusely. I smiled at him and said, "I made that decision a long time ago."

One of my mentors told me the story of bringing home a new can of paint to repaint a room in his house. Once he applied the first brush stroke of paint, he realized it was the wrong color for the room. He put the lid back on the can, and intended to return it for a full refund. Then this verse came into his mind: "A false balance is an abomination to the Lord" (Prov. 11:1). He told the truth when he went back to the store, and wound up getting a full refund and a new can of paint anyway. But that was the store's decision, not his. He was returning less than he had paid for, and didn't want to cheat even in a tiny thing.

While writing this chapter, I happened across a story about Marcus Henderson, a cashier at a Chick-fil-A restaurant in Lubbock, Texas. One day, a customer drove off, leaving behind three dollars in change. Rather than dumping it in the till, or sticking it in his pocket, he put it in an envelope and brought it with him to work every day. About a month later, the same customer returned to the restaurant, and Marcus gave him back his change.

It blew the guy away. He said, "What a breath of fresh air! I never would have missed it. It meant that much to him, so it meant even that much more to me." Marcus said it was just part of the job. "I'm called to serve these people well, not only because of my job but because of who I am. This has pushed me to act in ways where I wouldn't naturally."

"Unequal weights and unequal measures are both alike an abomination to the Lord." ~ Proverbs 20:10

"The wages of the righteous bring them life but the income of the wicked brings them punishment." ~ Proverbs 10:16 (NIV)

A FATHER'S PRAYER

Father, I pray for my son, that he will grow up by your grace to be a man of integrity in every part of his life. I pray that you will bless the labor of his hands all his life, that he may provide for his family and give to your kingdom work. In Jesus' name, amen.

Speech

CHAPTER 21

A real man controls his tongue; a boy doesn't.

"Death and life are in the power of the tongue, and those who love it will eat its fruits." ~ Proverbs 18:21

"A word fitly spoken is like apples of gold in a setting of silver." ~ Proverbs 25:11

When my son J.D. was about six or so, he was out in the backyard. I went out to fire up the grill, and I heard him talking while he was bouncing on the trampoline. I said, "J.D., are you talking to yourself?"

"Yes."

"You just trying to talk to somebody you can have an intelligent conversation with?"

"No," he said, as he kept bouncing. "I'm just trying to talk to somebody who understands what I'm saying."

He was learning at an early age the importance of mastering the use of the tongue.

According to the Bible, your tongue is the most difficult member of your body to control. "No human being can tame the tongue. It is a restless evil, full of deadly poison" (James 3:8). This simply means that you need God's help to control your speech. This is why the book of Proverbs talks more about the tongue than just about anything else.

The words you say have more power to heal and to destroy than you know. A word of encouragement can be something that someone else remembers for the rest of his life. A word of condemnation likewise can be a word that someone else never forgets. Poorly chosen words can rupture friendships beyond repair. "Reckless words pierce like a sword" (Prov. 12:18a, NIV). If you've ever had someone say cruel things to you, you know exactly what Solomon means.

A friend of mine who is now with the Lord, shared with me a story from the early days of his marriage. His wife had just started taking piano lessons. One day, as he listened to her plunk away, he made some crack about the quality of her play. It stung her so much that she immediately closed the lid on the piano and never played it again. He told me that story with tears in his eyes. The point here is to choose your words carefully and think before you speak.

I once went through a particularly difficult patch when prominent people were saying very critical things about what I had been saying in my effort to defend the truth of God's Word in the public arena, and no one was coming to my defense. It rocked my world pretty good and I barely survived. In the middle of that, while I was still reeling from the controversy, a friend of mine came into my office and shut the door. He sat down, looked me right in the eye, and said, "Keep doing what you're doing. We need your voice out there. Don't stop. Keep doing what you're doing." I can't tell you what a boost that word of reassurance was to me.

I told my friend later, "You know, there are very few things anybody has ever said to me that I will remember for the rest of my life, but that was one of them." It was just what I needed to hear to be encouraged to carry on despite all the hostility that was being directed at me. As Solomon says, "Anxiety in a man's heart weighs him down, but a good word makes him glad" (Prov. 12:25).

On another occasion, while I was on a backpacking trip in the Idaho wilderness with my daughter and some other dads and their daughters, I was struggling with fear, anxiety, and doubt about starting a new church from scratch. It was a venture I knew God was calling me to pursue, but I was coming up on the moment of truth when the church would begin, and I would be totally dependent on the kind of reception this start-up church would receive. My severance from my previous job was just about to run out, and I had no safety net.

When I slipped into my sleeping bag that night in our tent, I couldn't get to sleep. In fact, I experienced a full-blown panic attack. When people talk about panic attacks or anxiety attacks, I know exactly what they mean. Everything in me literally was screaming for me to strip off all my clothes and run screaming naked through the woods. This attack from Satan was so overpowering and overwhelming that I could not even pray. All I could do was quote Scripture out loud to Satan over and over: "The Lord is my rock and my fortress and my deliverer. The Lord is my rock and my fortress and my deliverer. The Lord is my rock and my fortress and my deliverer" (Ps. 18:2). Eventually the attack stopped suddenly, Satan fled, the panic subsided, and I was able to drift off to sleep. As the Bible says, "Resist the devil, and he will flee from you" (James 4:7).

The next morning, I shared my experience with one of the other fathers, a good buddy of mine, as we were standing on an overlook, viewing majestic mountains and high mountain lakes and beautiful blue skies. After I told my friend what had happened the previous night, he put his hand on my shoulder, waved his other hand over the spectacular scenery in front of me, and said, "Look at that, Bryan. The Lord doesn't make mistakes. You are going to be just fine." The words he spoke to me have stayed with me for decades. The Bible says, "The lips of the righteous nourish many" (Prov. 10:21a, NIV).

The Bible says, "Gracious words are like a honeycomb, sweetness to the soul and health to the body" (Prov. 16:24). Make it your objective in life to speak such words to others. Solomon says, "The mouth of the righteous is a fountain of life" (Prov. 10:11a).

On the other hand, cutting words you speak may wound someone for a long, long time. As I mentioned earlier, I once spoke a harsh word to someone in a Bible study, of all places. It was a word that seemed right to me at the time. But years later - 11 years to be exact - my conscience began to bother me about what I had said, and I had to track down the individual to whom I had spoken and seek forgiveness. I have painful memories of other words I have spoken in anger.

It's important not to blurt out the first thing that comes to mind, especially if you're worked up about it. "The heart of the righteous weighs its answers, but the mouth of the wicked gushes evil"(Prov. 15:28, NIV). The more you talk without thinking, the more damage you will do. "When words are many, sin is not absent, but he who holds his tongue is wise" (Prov. 10:19, NIV). But if you are careful about what you say, you will reap a reward."He who guards his lips guards his soul, but he who speaks rashly will come to ruin" (Prov. 13:3, NIV).

Don't talk about people behind their backs. Don't say anything negative about anybody unless that person is part of the problem you are trying to solve or part of the solution. "Whoever utters slander is a fool" (Prov. 10:18b).

Make it your ambition not to say hurtful words to or about others. In the next few years, you will have many opportunities to say cutting, snide, snarky things to or about other people, especially in response to snarky and cutting things they say to you. You can prevent a lot of arguments by not responding in kind. "A soft answer turns away wrath, but a harsh word stirs up anger" (Prov. 15:1).

You will also be tempted to make fun of people and to ridicule them for their appearance or their intelligence or their abilities or their mannerisms. Don't do it, even if everybody around you is. Using your mouth as an instrument of cruelty comes naturally to all of us, but it's a temptation you must learn to resist. "Whoever belittles his neighbor lacks sense, but a man of understanding remains silent" (Prov. 11:12).

If you're not sure the word you are about to speak is a word that builds others up rather than tears them down, it's best to say nothing at all until you can be sure.

Don't tell lies, and don't brag about yourself, even though you will find yourself tempted to insert things into a conversation that are only designed to impress other people about the wonder of you. "Let another praise you, and not your own mouth; someone else, and not your own lips" (Prov. 27:2, NIV).

You can start your path to maturity right now, by mastering how you speak to your parents, how you speak about them, and how you speak to your siblings. You can start right now to control your speech at school with your classmates.

I remember once being a counselor at a junior high summer camp. I hung out with my guys all week, and soon discovered that they liked to pick on other campers by ridiculing them for anything that made them different. I finally intervened and ordered them to stop. "Give the guy a break," I said. That became our cabin's watchword for the week. Anytime somebody would start in on another camper, the rest of us would chime in with, "Give the guy a break!"

Practice now speaking with respect to your peers - your friends and fellow students - and to those in authority. If you speak with respect to your teachers and coaches and bosses, somebody will likely accuse you of being a brown-noser. Ignore them and keep on doing the right thing. You will be developing habits of conversation that will be just what employers are looking for in the future.

Controlling your tongue will be essential in your working life and career. In fact, you will make more money with your tongue than anything else, including your brain. The way you speak to bosses, co-workers, clients, and customers will probably have more to do with your success than any other single thing. Solomon puts it this way: "From the fruit of his lips a man is filled with good things as surely as the work of his hands rewards him" (Prov. 12:14, NIV).

A man who demonstrates maturity through the control of his tongue and through the words that come out of his mouth soon gains a reputation as a man whom others can seek out for good counsel. It's a key to expanding your personal influence. Billy Graham was a noted preacher of the gospel, who presented the truths of God's Word before more people than any other man in human history. He spoke before millions, and had an impeccable reputation in the eyes of everyone. Because of his character and the way he used his lips to lift up and not tear down, it wasn't long before powerful men began to seek him out for spiritual counsel. He became a friend to 12 presidents and a close spiritual adviser to six of them. As Solomon says, "He who loves purity of heart, and whose speech is gracious, will have the king as his friend" (Prov. 22:11).

"Gold there is, and rubies in abundance, but lips that speak knowledge are a rare jewel." ~ Proverbs 20:15 (NIV)

A Father's Prayer

Father, I pray for my son, that he will guard his lips and so guard his life. I pray that no unwholesome word will come out of his mouth, but only words that are helpful for building others up, words that give grace to those who hear. Please use him to give timely counsel and encouragement to his friends. In Jesus' name, amen.

Finding God's Will for Your Life

CHAPTER 22

A real man seeks God's will for his life; a boy doesn't.

You have many important decisions ahead of you. What kind of education you pursue, what kind of career you pursue, whom you will marry, where you will live. Do I accept this job offer, or turn it down? Do I apply for a different job, or settle for the one I'm in? This job offer would involve a move; is that a wise thing at this point in my life or not?

One of my mentors made the observation that God has built life upside down. All the major decisions we make in life - like career and marriage - we must make when we are the least prepared to make them. We have to make life-critical decisions when we have less maturity and less life experience than we will ever have.

So how do we make good decisions in a circumstance like this? According to Solomon, there are two keys to making good life decisions when you are young: the first is to seek God with your whole heart, and the second is to seek godly counsel from mature men.

Proverbs 3:5-6 says, "Trust in the Lord with all your heart, and do not lean on your own understanding. In all your ways acknowledge him, and he will make straight your paths." God sees things that you don't, and so you need to place your trust in him without holding anything back. Now this doesn't mean you don't do your best to think through your options, and even develop an understanding about what you should do. But you are not to lean on your understanding, not place all your weight on your view of things.

You are to go to God, lay out your understanding of things, and ask him for his wisdom. If you do this, the promise of God is that "he will make your paths straight." He will point out to you the way you are to go. One of the implications of God's ability to "make your paths straight" is that he has the power to make a way for you when there seems to be no way. He can open doors for you that no man can shut, sometimes doors you didn't even know were there, and have a surprise waiting for you on the other side of that door.

For instance, I applied to Stanford University because I wanted to get the best education I could get. Now there's nothing wrong with that, and God opened that door for me. But I realize now, looking back, that while my purpose for going to college was to get an education, God's purpose was to call me into ministry.

As I mentioned earlier, while in college I was discipled by strong, mature, Christlike men. But I also had the privilege of attending an outstanding Bible church, Peninsula Bible Church, where for the first time I was exposed to masculine Christianity. That church made the ministry appealing to me, because it was the first time I'd been in a church that I wanted to be a part of, a church that was the kind of church I realized I might want to pastor some day.

The churches I had been involved in growing up seemed to practice a kind of Christianity that was soft, almost feminine in nature, and made Christianity seem like something that was for women and not for strong, bold, masculine men. But PBC was different. It was led by mature men, and it emphasized the expository teaching of the Bible, that is, going through books of the Bible verse by verse, rather than topical

Bible teaching. That was the kind of Bible teaching I wanted to do. I began leading Bible studies in college, and since most of my mentors there had gone to Dallas Theological Seminary, that's where I decided to go. I couldn't have seen any of that when I enrolled. But that's exactly why we need to trust in the Lord with all our heart.

God has directed the course of my life through open doors and closed doors more than in any other way. When I was about halfway through seminary, I wanted to quit and get started in ministry. I'd gotten what I went to Dallas to get, a grounding in the biblical languages of Hebrew and Greek, and I was ready to rock and roll. But God seemed to be holding me back, and I finally made a deal with him: I'd stay right where I was unless he opened a door for me to leave. He didn't. So I slogged it out for two more years, and by the end of two years, when I graduated, he had opened up a spot for me at a solid, Bible teaching church in Boise, Idaho, where I could serve under one of the men who had mentored me in college. It was that position that set the trajectory of my career, and I would have missed that if I'd jumped ship when I wanted to. And it truly was a "straight path." We loaded up the UHaul two days after graduation and hit the road to Boise. The truth is that I couldn't have found Boise on a map if my life depended on it, but that was clearly where God wanted us.

In fact, the best answer to prayer I have ever gotten from God is "No." He's the only one who sees the end from the beginning, and when his answer is "No," either he is protecting me from something or saving me for something better.

Don't be afraid to knock on doors. Don't be afraid to apply for a job you'd really like. Don't let timidity and fear stop you.

Go right ahead and apply, remember this advice from Solomon: "The plans of the heart belong to man, but the answer of the tongue is from the Lord." Your job is to apply; the answer you get is from the Lord, not from man. God can't steer a parked car, so keep moving and trust God to lead you to the place he wants you to be. As Solomon says, "The heart of man plans his way, but the Lord establishes his steps" (Prov. 16:9). It's the plan that comes from God's heart that we want, not the one that comes from our own heart. And if we trust him, he will lead us into the plan that comes from his heart.

Sometimes we have to learn the hard way that not all of our ideas, as brilliant as they may seem to us, are from God. The failure of one of our plans isn't really a failure - it's just God's way of saying, "That just wasn't something I wanted you to do." This is how Solomon puts it, "There is no wisdom, no insight, no plan that can succeed against the LORD" (Prov. 21:30, NIV).

Thomas Edison was one of history's great inventors. We owe the light bulb to his genius. But it didn't come easy. He tried one creative idea after another that fell short. Someone asked him one time how it felt to fail so often in that task. He said, "I have not failed. I've just found 10,000 ways that won't work."

So pursue things that are in your heart, and trust that God will winnow away those things that are not in his plan for your life. As Solomon says, "Many are the plans in the mind of a man, but it is the purpose of the Lord that will stand" (Prov. 19:21).

Sometimes when God closes a door, it slams closed on your foot and it can hurt. But God uses closed doors to tell us that it's time for a change. When I resigned from my first ministry assignment because of differences in philosophy and direction, it hurt. I left behind a job and people I loved and a bright and secure future. But it was that closed door that opened the door to found a church which I pastored for 12 years.

Then that door closed when I got fired, over a difference in understanding of the biblical qualifications for leadership. That too was brutal. I'd never in my life been fired from anything. But that painful experience opened the door for me to begin a pro-family organization in my state and the opportunity to lead a successful statewide effort to protect God's definition of marriage in our state constitution. And my work with that pro-family organization led to the opportunity to join the American Family Association and the best job I've ever had, that of being a radio talk show host.

It also led to a move to Tupelo, Mississippi, another town I couldn't have found on a map if my life depended on it. I knew it was the birthplace of Elvis Presley, but I had absolutely no idea where it was. In fact, if you had asked me to list the 500 places I'd be most likely to never live in, Tupelo would have been at the top of the list.

I could never have foreseen or predicted the path that my life has taken. As one of my mentors told me, "Life must be lived forward, but can only be understand backward." You often cannot see what God is doing when he's in the middle of doing it. That's why we must trust God with every day of our lives. That's why Solomon is exactly right when he says, "A man's steps are from the Lord; how then can man understand his way?" (Prov. 20:24).

I've also learned that the worst things that have ever happened to me in my life are the best things that have ever happened to me. God was using the heartache and anguish and disappointment of each painful thing to prepare me for an important and very beneficial change in my life. He will do the same for you.

And don't forget, especially if you wind up in a leadership position, to seek counsel from wise, mature men in your circle of friends. It's not that they will all agree. It's more that one of them may offer just the perspective you need to keep you from making a bad decision or to help you make a good one. Solomon puts it this way, "Without counsel plans fail, but with many advisers they succeed" (Prov. 15:22).

If you want to develop a successful career, Solomon has one major piece of advice: work hard, and do every job as well as you possibly can. There are a lot of gifted people who are failures because they thought they could get by on talent alone. They were in a hurry to get rich, and didn't realize that a satisfying career is built one small success at a time. Here's how Solomon puts it: "The plans of the diligent lead surely to abundance, but everyone who is hasty comes only to poverty" (Prov. 21:5).

Promotions and advances in your career come from using every opportunity to get as good at your job as you can get. "Do you see a man skillful in his work? He will stand before kings; he will not stand before obscure men" (Prov. 22:29). Now I've never stood before kings, but I have had, by God's grace, the opportunity to stand before city councils, mayors, legislatures, and governors. I've even had the privilege of serving as the chaplain of our state senate, standing before these lawmakers and leading them each day in prayer. Don't forget Billy Graham - he was a farm boy who followed God and wound up being a counselor to six presidents.

Do your work diligently and trust God to elevate you in his time and in his way. He won't let you down.

"Trust in the Lord with all your heart, and do not lean on your own understanding. Acknowledge him in all your ways, and he will make straight your paths." ~ Proverbs 3:5-6

A Father's Prayer

Heavenly Father, I pray that your hand of favor will rest on my son his entire life. Guide him at each step of his journey. Show him the gifts and abilities you have given him, and enable him to develop them to the full. Open doors before him that no man can shut, and fulfill every purpose you have for his life. In Jesus' name, amen.

Politics

CHAPTER 23

A real man cares about politics; a boy doesn't.

Politics is always a controversial subject. But still God's men must be concerned about politics for one simple reason: God is.

Politics is God's idea, not man's. God is the one who invented government, and every bit of authority any politician exercises has been delegated to him by God. As the Scriptures say, "There is no authority except from God, and those that exist have been established by God" (Rom. 13:1). God's men are not opposed to government; we are just opposed to government that is too big, takes too much of our income in taxes, and abuses its power.

Now just because the authority itself comes from God does not mean that everything an elected official does must meet with our approval. While a man's political authority may come from God, his actions may not. It's part of our responsibility as men to be discerning about what our elected officials do, and evaluate what they do by stacking it up against the standards of the Word of God.

When governing officials do that which is right in God's eyes, we commend them. When they do things that are wrong in God's eyes, we criticize them. In politics, as in all things, the Scriptures serve as our guide.

Some people say that Christians should never criticize our president, for instance, because he has been put in place by God. But if that is true, then God is the biggest offender. He placed the kings of ancient Israel on the throne, but at the same time he raised up prophets to hold them accountable for God's standard of governing. When a king did what was right in the eyes of the Lord, the prophets praised him. When the king did what was evil in the eyes of the Lord, the prophets condemned him.

Some people say that godly men should not be involved in politics. Again, if this is true, then God is the biggest offender. He raised up one man of faith after another and put them in positions of political leadership. Moses was the greatest lawgiver in history, and one of the great political leaders of all time. He brought a nation into existence, gave its people liberty, and took them to the land in which they were to live. He was followed by the judges, who were both political leaders and military commanders, and they in turn were followed by King Saul, then King David, then all the sons of David who sat on his throne. In fact, if we got rid of all the parts of Scripture that feature a political leader as a central character, we'd be left with the first 37 chapters of Genesis, the book of Ruth, and a few of the Psalms. We'd lose about 80% of the Bible in the process.

When people say that Christian men should not be involved in government, they seem to be blind to the reality that the only alternative is to leave it in the hands of atheists - people who don't believe in God - and other leaders who couldn't care less about God or His standards for culture and society. That's a great example of a really bad idea.

Some people even try to say that Jesus was not involved in politics. But the truth is that Jesus was involved in politics almost every day of His earthly ministry. His main adversaries were the Sadducees and the Pharisees, and while it is true they were religious leaders, they were politicians as well. They made laws that governed even the details of people's lives, down to how far they could walk on Saturdays, how they were required to wash up before dinner, and how much they had to pay in taxes.

When Jesus confronted them, he called them "a brood of vipers," that is, a bunch of slimy, poisonous snakes. He was confronting them not just in their role as spiritual leaders but also as political leaders. They often made laws that enabled them to rip off poor people of what little they had and use it to line their own pockets. So Jesus was involved in politics. And since he is our example, we must be involved in politics, too.

It's important that, as God's men, we use our influence, whether it's our vote or our voice, to put godly men in office. Our concern must not just be for ourselves but for our nation. As Solomon says, "Righteousness exalts a nation, but sin is a reproach to any people" (Prov. 14:34). When a nation embraces and celebrates sin, that nation is weakened and its moral character erodes.

Become not only a student of the Bible but of the Declaration of Independence and the Constitution as well. The Declaration identifies the rights that are a gift to us from God. The first of these are life, liberty, and property (the Founding Fathers used the expression, "the pursuit of happiness" for property). These rights, because they are gifts to us from the Creator, are "inalienable." That means that no man and no government has the moral authority to take them away from us.

The purpose of government is not to give us our rights, but to protect the rights that have already been given to us by God. The first right the Founders identified in the

Constitution that government has a sacred duty to protect is the right to the "free exercise" of our Christian faith. This right is under constant attack, as Christians have been fired and Christian-run businesses have been closed by a government that often punishes faith rather than protecting it. As you emerge into adulthood, you will soon realize that the greatest threat to religious liberty in our day comes from the radical homosexual movement, which demands that any citizen who won't affirm homosexual behavior must be punished in some way.

So we must use our influence to work toward a nation that embraces righteousness rather than sin. The Bible teaches us that every life is sacred, so we must oppose abortion with every fiber of our being. Abortion is nothing less than the murder of a tiny, little human being in its earliest stages of development. No nation has a long future which embraces the slaughter of babies. Even though abortion is widely practiced in our nation, it doesn't have to be this way forever. We must never give up working for the day when every baby in the womb of his mother is protected by the law. As Solomon says, "Rescue those who are being taken away to death; hold back those who are stumbling to the slaughter" (Prov. 24:11).

And we can't afford to ignore this issue or pretend we don't know how serious it is. "If you say, 'Behold, we did not know this,' does not he who weighs the heart perceive it? Does not he who keeps watch over your soul know it, and will he not repay man according to his work?" (Prov. 24:12). We may not be able to stop abortion in our generation, but we must all do whatever we can to advance the cause of life.

The Bible teaches us that marriage is the foundation of civilization and that any society that does not honor marriage as God has designed it and defined it is headed for the trash heap of history. Remember what happened to Sodom and Gomorrah, two cities which celebrated homosexuality instead of turning from it.

Marriage is exclusively the union of one man and one woman. As the second page of the Bible says, "For this reason, a man (note: one man) shall leave his father and mother and hold fast to his wife (note: one woman) and the two (note: not three or four) shall become one flesh" (Genesis 2:24). Do not let our culture and our media convince you that two men or two women can form a marriage. They can't.

Our society has in large measure embraced both homosexuality and homosexual "marriage," but our calling must be to oppose this and work for the day when marriage will once again be reserved only for what God calls marriage. And we must work for the day when homosexual behavior will once again be understood to be something that deviates from God's design for sexual expression and something which no rational culture should ever promote or celebrate.

George Washington, our first commander-in-chief, once dismissed a man from the Continental Army because he attempted to engage in homosexual sex with another soldier. And he did it quite publicly. He had the entire army line up in two rows, then had all his drummers beat on the drums while the disgraced soldier marched out of his army while all the rest of Washington's soldiers looked on. He understood, as we have already mentioned, that "righteousness exalts a nation, but sin is a reproach to any people" (Prov. 14:34).

As God's men, we must oppose a government that transfers responsibility from the individual and the family to government. We will support lower taxes, to make it easier for a husband and father to support his family. We will oppose a government that grows too large and regulates too much of life, for the larger government gets, the less freedom and liberty we will possess. The bigger the government, the smaller the citizen. Solomon puts it this way, "Like a roaring lion or a charging bear is a wicked ruler over a poor people" (Prov. 28:15).

So it's important that you even now begin to pay attention to politics and learn to identify which candidates for office you can support. Look for men who have a reverence for God and will support biblical values in public policy. As Solomon says, "Evil men do not understand justice, but those who seek the Lord understand it completely" (Prov. 28:5).

If we learn to put godly men in office, everybody will benefit. If we put ungodly men in office, everybody will suffer. "When the righteous triumph, there is great elation; but when the wicked rise to power, men go into hiding" (Prov. 28:12, NIV). The more evil government gets, the worse it is for righteous men.

But on the other hand, if we use our influence to put mature, godly men into power, the better it is for everybody. "When the righteous increase, the people rejoice, but when the wicked rule, the people groan" (Prov. 29:2).

Our president is the commander-in-chief of our armed forces. We must work to elect a president whose ultimate trust is not in our military but in God. "The horse is made ready for the day of battle, but the victory belongs to the Lord" (Prov. 21:31). Most of our presidents have understood this. One of the most famous paintings from the Revolutionary War is of George Washington, our first commander-in-chief, kneeling in prayer in the snow at Valley Forge. President

Franklin Roosevelt went on national radio on June 6, 1944, and personally led the entire nation in a six-and-a-half minute prayer for our troops as they prepared to attack the beaches of Normandy.

We want a president who knows God and seeks his guidance, for that president can be led by God. As Solomon puts it, "The king's heart is in the hand of the Lord; he directs it like a watercourse wherever he pleases" (Prov. 21:1, NIV).

George Washington said, "Of all the dispositions and habits which lead to political prosperity, religion (by which he meant Christianity) and morality (by which he meant the Ten Commandments) are indispensable supports." "Indispensable" means absolutely necessary. We cannot have a prosperous nation without them. In fact, he added that no man can be a patriot who refuses to accept this. "In vain would that man claim the tribute of patriotism who labors to subvert these great pillars of human happiness."

As one of our Founding Fathers, John Adams said, "Our Constitution was made only for a moral and religious People. It is wholly inadequate to the government of any other." Anybody who tells you anything different doesn't know what he is talking about.

A FATHER'S PRAYER

Heavenly Father, I pray that you will cause my son to grow up to be a patriot who not only loves you but our nation as well. Grant him discernment, and motivate him to use his influence to turn this nation back to you and your standards. In Jesus' name, amen.

Standing Alone

CHAPTER 24

A real man can stand alone; a boy can't.

"The wicked flee when no one pursues, but the righteous are bold as a lion." ~ Proverbs 28:1

Some men are scaredy cats, who are so timid and jumpy that "the sound of a driven leaf shall put them to flight" (Lev. 26:36). Other men in the same circumstances have the fortitude and inner strength to stand tall, firm, and immovable in the face of danger. That's the kind of man God wants you to be.

There won't be too many times in your life when you will face a choice between standing for principle or caving to pressure. But those times will come and they will represent your greatest tests of character, and be the defining moments in your life.

I've only been fired twice in my life. In both cases, the issue turned on a matter of Scripture and deep internal principle, a matter on which I could not simply go along with everybody else without violating both God's word and my own conscience. You need to think now about how you will respond when it's your turn in the barrel.

The pressure to compromise your principles might be immense. Everyone around you may be capitulating and leaning on you to do the same. Important and even powerful people might be bringing their weight to bear on you. Close friends might betray you because they have already decided to surrender. If you stand firm, you may have to stand alone.

I'd like to finish by telling you about one of my all-time heroes, a man by the name of Athanasius. He was a leader in the church in the 4th century A.D., at a time when there was great debate about the nature of Christ, the Son of God. Was he made of a different substance than the Father, a similar substance, or the same substance? If Jesus is truly God, as the Bible teaches, then he is made of the same substance as the Father. They are both equally God in their very being. This is what Athanasius believed.

A man by the name of Arius believed the error that Jesus was not truly God, but was instead the first thing that God made. Now if Jesus was not truly God, then he could not offer a sacrifice of eternal value for you and me, and we would have no forgiveness of sins and no promise of eternal life. So everything was riding on what the church chose to believe.

Arius was persuasive enough that he got many church leaders and even several Roman emperors to believe his heresy. In fact, Athanasius was forced into hiding or driven from the Empire completely no less than five times by emperors and church leaders who had gotten sucked into the heresy of Arius. Six different times he was forced to flee his home town of Alexandria, Egypt, to avoid teams of assassins sent to kill him. There were many times when Athanasius stood alone for the truth about Christ.

One time, when Athanasius was in exile, rejected by the emperor and the church alike, one of his disciples said to him, "Athanasius, the whole world is against you." His immortal reply: "Then Athanasius is against the whole world."

He found strength in God to stand without flinching or wavering against the mightiest power in the world because he refused to compromise the truth of the Word of God. He was as bold as a lion.

And he was vindicated in the end. Today his view that Christ is the eternal and divine Son of God is accepted in all Bible-centered churches as the truth. But the battle nearly cost him his life and did cost him his freedom.

There are many biblical truths that have been rejected today by influential people in our world. People who take a stand for the truth in today's world often find themselves the victims of rejection, ridicule, hatred, and even violence. Many followers of Christ have lost jobs and businesses because they have refused the pressure and threats of the world to compromise.

The world rejects the truth that the universe was created by God rather than evolving from nothing. It rejects the truth that marriage is exclusively the union of one man and one woman. It rejects the truth that homosexuality is a sin in God's eyes. It rejects the truth that there are only two genders, male and female, and not dozens, as some deceived people want us to believe. It rejects the truth that a pregnant woman carries a baby in her womb and not just a clump of tissue.

In high school, college, and beyond, you may find yourself in settings where virtually no one who is willing to speak will admit that they believe the Bible rather than the world. You will be where Athanasius was, in a place where it seems as though the whole world is against you.

It was a long, nasty, and brutal struggle, but Athanasius prevailed in the end. Here is the question for you: When you find that the whole world is against you, will you be able to say, with Athanasius, "Then I am against the whole world?"

A FATHER'S PRAYER

Father, I pray that you will infuse my son with great inner strength by your Holy Spirit. May he be a man of courage and boldness who does not wilt or bend even in the face of the strongest wind. May he be like an oak of righteousness and stand for you and your truth without compromise or capitulation. In the name of Jesus, amen.

The Ceremony of the Five Stones

A number of years ago, I had the privilege of going on a tour of the Holy Land. We went to the valley where David confronted and defeated Goliath. David took five smooth stones from the creek in the middle of the valley. Now he only needed one, but perhaps he picked up enough to take care of Goliath's brothers. He put one stone in his sling, fired it at Goliath, hit him square in the middle of his forehead, and Goliath fell down dead.

I picked up five smooth stones from that same creek and brought them home. For J.D.'s 16th birthday, I put them in a small leather pouch and invited four other mature Christian men, besides myself, to come to our home one evening for a little ceremony I had prepared. Each was a man who had played an important role in my son's life. One man was a family friend J.D. looked up to, another was his martial arts instructor, a third was our worship leader, who had incorporated J.D. into our church worship team, and the fourth was the Young Life leader who had taken J.D. under his wing and mentored him. I gave each man one of the stones, with a Bible verse to read over J.D. as he gave him the stone. At the end of the little ceremony, we all laid hands on him and prayed for him as he continued his journey to full manhood.

THE CEREMONY OF THE FIVE STONES
For Jonathan David Fischer
On the occasion of your sixteenth birthday, February 10, 2000

When David faced the giant Goliath, he went into battle armed with five stones. The qualities of character listed below are symbolically the five stones you are to carry with you as you move into manhood and prepare for the challenges every man must face in life. If you arm yourself with these, you will be able to face every challenge and emerge from battle victorious and triumphant. And you will have the confidence that when your earthly life ends and you stand before your Lord to be judged, you will hear him say, "Well done, good and faithful servant."

INTEGRITY - PSALM 15
To act with character even when no one is looking

LORD, who may dwell in your sanctuary?
Who may live on your holy hill?

He whose walk is blameless and who does what is righteous,
Who speaks the truth from his heart and has no
slander on his tongue,
Who does his neighbor no wrong and casts no
slur on his fellowman,
Who despises a vile man but honors those
who fear the LORD,
Who keeps his oath even when it hurts,
Who lends his money without usury and does not
accept a bribe against the innocent.

He who does these things will never be shaken.

COURAGE – JOSHUA 1:9
To face every challenge without flinching or whining

Have I not commanded you? Be strong and courageous. Do not be terrified; do not be discouraged, for the LORD your God will be with you wherever you go.

FAITH – ROMANS 4:18-21
To trust God to do impossible things through you

Against all hope, Abraham in hope believed…He did not waver through unbelief regarding the promise of God, but was strengthened in his faith and gave glory to God, being fully persuaded that God had power to do what he had promised.

LOYALTY – PROVERBS 17:17, 18:24
To be a faithful and trustworthy friend

A friend loves at all times, and a brother is born for adversity.

A man of many companions may come to ruin, But there is a friend who sticks closer than a brother.

PURITY – 1 THESSALONIANS 4:3,4,7
To walk with purity in word, thought, and deed

It is God's will that you should be sanctified: that you should avoid sexual immorality; that each of you should learn to control his own body in a way that is holy and honorable. For God did not call us to be impure, but to live a holy life.

IF

If you can keep your head when all about you
Are losing theirs and blaming it on you;
If you can trust yourself when all men doubt you,
But make allowance for their doubting too
If you can wait and not be tired by waiting,
Or, being lied about, don't deal in lies,
Or, being hated, don't give way to hating,
And yet don't look too good, nor talk too wise;

If you can dream – and not make dreams your master;
If you can think – and not make thoughts your aim;
If you can meet with triumph and disaster
And treat those two impostors just the same;

If you can bear to hear the truth you've spoken
Twisted by knaves to make a trap for fools,
Or watch the things you gave your life to broken,
And stoop and build 'em up with worn out tools;

If you can make one heap of all your winnings
And risk it on one turn of pitch-and-toss,
And lose, and start again at your beginnings
And never breathe a word about your loss;

If you can force your heart and nerve and sin
To serve your turn long after they are gone,
And so hold on when there is nothing in you
Except the will which says to them: "Hold on";

If you can talk with crowds and keep your virtue,
Or walk with kings – nor lose the common touch;
If neither foes nor loving friends can hurt you;
If all men count with you, but none too much;

If you can fill the unforgiving minute
With sixty seconds' worth of distance run
Yours is the Earth and everything that's in it,
And – which is more – you'll be a Man, my son!
~ Rudyard Kipling ~

MY PRAYER FOR MY SON ON HIS 16TH BIRTHDAY

Adapted from General Douglas MacArthur's prayer for his son

Build me a son, oh Lord, who will be strong enough to know when he is weak, and brave enough to face himself when he is afraid; one who will be proud and unbending in honest defeat, and humble and gentle in victory.

Build me a son whose wishes will not take the place of deeds, a son who will know you – and that to know you is the foundation stone of knowledge.

Lead him, I pray, not in the path of ease and comfort but under the stress and spur of difficulties and challenge. Here let him learn to stand up in the storm; here let him learn compassion for those who fail.

Build me a son whose heart will be clear, whose goals will be high, a son who will master himself before he seeks to master other men, one who will reach into the future yet never forget the past.

And after all these things are his, add, I pray, enough of a sense of humor so that he may always be serious, yet never take himself too seriously. Give him humility, so that he may always remember the simplicity of true greatness, the open mind of true wisdom, and the meekness of true strength.

Then I, his father, will dare to whisper, "I have not lived in vain." In Jesus' name, Amen

From this day forward, we, the undersigned, accept J.D. Fischer into the fraternity of adult males. We will no longer regard him as a boy but as a man, and we will expect him to conduct himself as a man. We pledge ourselves to set a mature, Christlike example of manhood for him to imitate.